AN AMERICAN IN ART

IN ART

A Professional and Technical Autobiography

AN AMERICAN IN ART

The University Press of Kansas
Lawrence, Manhattan, Wichita, London

A Professional and Technical Autobiography

Thomas Hart Benton (signature)

including his
"American Regionalism: A Personal History of the Movement"

"American Regionalism: A Personal History of the Movement"
is from The University of Kansas City Review,
Volume XVIII, Number 1 (Autumn 1951).
Copyright 1951 by the University of Kansas City.
Used by permission of the University of Kansas City.

Design by Fritz Reiber
Photograph of Thomas Hart Benton, 1968, by James Enyeart

to Rita

who
knows
all
about
the
most
of
this

CONTENTS

Benton's Contribution to American Art

by Earle Davis

It is simple to say that Thomas Hart Benton is a great American artist! It is tempting to be hyperbolic if you are interested in literature as well as art, for Benton approaches mastery of words as well as pigment and design. He serves as a kind of modern Benvenuto Cellini, except that he writes more effectively and entertainingly than Cellini. Benton's first autobiography is called *An Artist in America*, and a very recent edition of it brings the original story up-to-date.

Now he has written another autobiography, this time concentrating on the development of his artistic techniques and intentions in his paintings and murals. For many readers this new narrative is even more fascinating than the earlier one, although the two stories must be considered as complementing each other. His writing reminds us that he is more than an artist, more than a mere "regionalist" who can be classed with Grant Wood and John Steuart Curry or other painters concentrating on some part of the American scene. He is a genius who furnishes an American Ethos, one who records memorably and for eternity the way we Americans look, think, and act.

Just about a hundred years ago Walt Whitman published the first part of an essay he eventually called "Democratic Vistas." His purpose was to praise and define that which is and should be distinctly American, something separate from the European or the traditional or the decadent, something not only great and good and new, but also our very own.

> I say that democracy can never prove itself beyond cavil, until it founds and luxuriantly grows its own forms of art, poems, schools, theology, displacing all that exists, or that has been produced anywhere in the past, under opposite influences . . . . Our fundamental want today in the United States . . . is of a class, and the clear idea of a class, of native authors, literatuses, far different, far higher in grade, than any yet known . . . permeating the whole mass of American mentality, taste, belief, breathing into it a new breath of life . . . .

Whether or not America can develop something unique in artistic matters is a question which has haunted our country for most of our history. Whitman's patriotic excesses have often been ignored or toned down by our critics in favor of some international or universal artistic standard. We have also had natural difficulties in being completely American because of the facts of our heritage. We began with ineradicable debts to our fore-fathers who came not only from many nations and races, but mostly from cultures which had already produced great examples of literature, art, and music. Most newer nations have perforce imitated and adapted their artistic creeds from the models already established as great. Imitation suffers from twofold difficulties. It constricts the focus and scope of the creative talent in new surroundings, and it is rarely as good as the originals which inspire the imitation. Poetry, music, and painting in America have long struggled to escape the strangling bonds of adaptation on the one hand and the strict standards imposed by other lands and cultures on the other.

Consider the example of Whitman himself. He tried to be American by excluding his technical past, that is he abandoned the traditional rhyth-mical and rhyming forms which had characterized poetry in the tradition of the Western World. Other nineteenth-century poets like Longfellow tried to be distinctively American through the use of native subject matter treated in the manner which had been traditional in English or European poetry. Longfellow borrowed the form of the Finnish epic *Kalevala* for his *Hiawatha* and the dactylic hexameter of the Greek and Latin epics for *Evangeline*, whether or not they were completely appropriate couplings. Occasionally someone like Lowell would experiment with American dialect (as in *The Biglow Papers*) to reach a particular American public, and others like Whittier began tentatively to borrow from the simple American folk-manner. In the twentieth century, poets like Carl Sandburg and Robert Frost have tried to be distinctly American in language and technique, but most modern poets have developed their art in terms of a European, foreign, or universally English tradition, whatever its debts to a strictly American viewpoint.

Music and Art have had similar problems. Charles Ives might compose a symphony in the general manner of Brahms, but utilize American hymns, folk songs, and patriotic tunes as his themes. From John Singleton Copley through Thomas Eakins, Winslow Homer, and George Caleb Bingham, American artists attempted to explore American subject matter with some degree of individualistic realism and therefore to establish a distinctive American tradition. Most of these artists have achieved recognition much later than sooner, Ives waiting almost till he was dead before he heard a great American orchestra play one of his major compositions, Homer and Eakins achieving twentieth-century attention long after they were alive or able to appreciate popular interest and recognition.

Benton, of course, has had experiences which coincide with those of many great artists in other countries and times. The delayed response of the public to artistic accomplishment is perhaps peculiar to our capitalistic world, but artists who die poor are often bad managers of their own finances. Paintings are more valuable after their creator's death because there is no more work that can be produced by that artist, and collectors must bid against each other for possession of what exists. Sometimes the value of paintings depends upon the critical reception given the artist in his lifetime. Benton has lived long enough to be very popular and also to suffer criticism from those who are modernist in some degree, perhaps followers of the great Paris-inspired *isms*, or the developers of the abstract rather than the realistic. He has contributed to artistic quarrels by attacking volubly everything from precious to symbolic to hard-to-understand art, from communism to stupid patriotism. He has been a good fighter, and he knows that his eventual status in the total record of art will depend upon what he has accomplished with his genius and his own artistic aims rather than whether his way of painting is *ipso facto* better than other approaches.

But he is not an irenical man. He has something to say, even if he does not believe that art should be interpreted in terms of "message." For example he insists that "native art" is not by definition "good art." Realistic American painting, in whatever form it is produced, has been subject to advertising and commercial pressures, to photographic techniques, even to folksy representations like those of Grandma Moses. Benton says:

> It [native art] became good for the rising trade of advertising and an instrument of its hoopla salesmanship which, as business spokesmen said, was in line with the new Protestant image of Christ. Here art found its first real and recognized public function in America. Here also it was degraded as no art has ever been in the history of the world. Along with fraudulent verbiage, a fraudulent, retouched photographic type of realism was erected which gave to all realism a suggestion of sham.

Trying to define his kind of realism we call him a "regionalist." Professional art critics seem to find something limiting or even derogatory in the term itself, as if concentration on the life, land, and social behavior of a part of the United States were somehow an inferior condition of creative composition. We recall that for a long time William Faulkner suffered from this judgment in the reception of his novels about Yoknapatawpha County in Mississippi. The great creative artist in any sector must obviously transcend his subject matter and make it universal by his interpretation of it. Surely it is appropriate that Benton has furnished illustrations for several of the great regionalist novels of Mark Twain, among them *Tom Sawyer* and *Huckleberry Finn*.

Benton's new artistic biography details the artist's search for the way to glory. Most of us have trouble in understanding the ways of painters in transferring their inspiration to canvas, and this difficulty is often complicated by the jargon used by critics in any special field. For example Benton is supposed to have "developed an intellectual style," the critical assumption being that it is too intellectual for his subject matter. He also is said to have filled his canvases with "undulating manneristic proportions, mathematically balanced." He was eclectic and "related a kind of Renaissance style to anthropomorphic cubism." He also used "calligraphic outlines (like Matisse) and sometimes elongated the proportions of his figures in the style of El Greco."

These descriptions are not untypical samples of what the critics say, but Benton does not talk this way at all. He makes his story of how he developed his theories and practice of painting seem like a great American adventure that anyone can understand without technical knowledge of a special kind. Somehow the paintings begin to take on new dimensions as we find out more about what he was trying to do.

His story is complicated by his attitude toward what is worth celebrating in America. Although he does not believe that painting is a propaganda vehicle for verbal messages, his selection of materials becomes in some degree didactic. He has painted what he thinks is important about our country, the life and condition of the poorer classes, the mines, the steel mills, the industry centers of the nation, the plains, the hillbilly mountain regions, the folksy countryside, the farms and cattle country, the religion of the simple people rather than the rich, the Negro and Indian, in other words "the people and the land." He depicts everything from folk ballads to universal myths, from Persephone to Susannah, from Huck Finn to Frankie and Johnny. The comparison to Sandburg is inevitable; his subject has been "The People, Yes."

For the non-special audience Benton's selection of material has been the beginning of argument. His murals have sometimes attracted aroused attention because he focused on subjects which many viewers would rather ignore or forget. In the Middle West anyone who is old enough to re-member must recall the hullabaloo which followed the exhibition of his mural in the Capitol of Missouri at Jefferson City, the placing of Huck Finn and Nigger Jim, Frankie and Johnny, even Boss Pendergast in prominent places on the wall commemorating Missouri's history. What most people claimed to want was a monument, not a challenge, certainly not the living soul of Missouri.

It is of incidental interest to Kansans that Benton's example came be-fore Curry's opportunity to do something of the same order in the Capitol at Topeka. Anxious Kansans apparently made sure that Curry painted nothing arguable after his striking study of John Brown, censoring such possible topics as Carrie Nation, or Dodge City, or Wild Bill Hickok for mural immortality. Instead we got placid farmers and cows, completely representative and common. The great regionalist trio, Benton, Wood, and Curry, were great because they wanted to interpret the importance of their land whenever they were permitted to do so. Wood's experiences with his Iowa Gothic and his sarcastic picture of the Daughters of the American Revolution show that he was a proper member of the fraternity.

Whatever the selection or emphasis, Benton's America is memorable. He reminds all Americans that maybe Walt Whitman was right. There is evidence that Benton may be the prophetic illustration of Walt's vision about someone really American who is really great too, and not necessarily in the crushing traditions of imitation and borrowed foreign standards. Those of us who love Tom Benton devoutly believe in him.

Manhattan, Kansas
October, 1968

6

AN AMERICAN IN ART

IN ART

A Professional and Technical Autobiography

AN AMERICAN IN ART

A Professional and Technical Autobiography

One of the commonest complaints about *An Artist in America** is that it provides too sketchy an account of my technical development. Letters from students and writers about art keep coming to me, asking for more specific information about this. They want to know in detail about the methods and artistic directions adopted at a given time and the reasons therefor. With the new interest of historians in the America of the twenties and thirties, this questioning has accelerated.

An Artist in America, as the title implies, is primarily a story of my adventures in America. As an artist's story it also necessarily involved some adventures in art, but these are secondary to the book's main purpose and are told about with as few specifically technical references as possible.

People in general do not care much about the methods an artist uses to arrive at his art. They are more interested in what that art brings to them in terms of meaning. *An Artist in America* was written for people in general and by an artist who had come to feel that the engagement of their interests and understanding had top priority.

Nevertheless the students and historians of art—those who ponder, explain, and theorize about artistic individuals, movements, and periods—have some right to the special information needed for their specialized pursuits. The methods an artist employs as he develops do have a great deal to do with what he delivers for public consumption. The history of how, when, and why he adopted certain methods rather than others is therefore necessary for a com-

---

* Thomas Hart Benton, *An Artist in America* (new and amplified edition, University of Missouri Press, 1968).

plete understanding of his career, though I do not believe for a complete response to what comes to be his art.

So, to compensate for the technical omissions of *An Artist in America*, I have prepared the following account. It does not change but amplifies that book. It will also repeat some of what has been told, but with a different emphasis— a technical emphasis. It assumes that the reader is at least moderately familiar with the history of art in this century and in preceding ones. To describe, explain, and document all that is referred to would take not pages but volumes.

Absorbed always during my life with problems of the day and generally with no great thought of the morrow, I have never bothered to keep scrapbooks or records. I have never treasured letters, catalogues of, or articles about, my work. From the archivists' point of view this is unpardonable, and I now do realize that I should have been more careful about such things. For many years I did not even sign or date my pictures. For a lot of them, therefore, the very time of their execution can only be approximately determined.

So this technical survey had to be written entirely from memory and without documentary support. Pure memory, I realize, cannot produce a completely detailed factual report. Our tendency to organize facts so they can be related to one another makes us suppress or leave out some of them. The complete truth, if it can be remembered at all, is chaotic and at times illogical, even completely nonsensical. It is also unmanageable.

What follows, then, is a *selection* of facts which stick in my memory as the *main* facts. In describing them I have done my best to avoid hindsight evaluations, though obviously some of this is inescapable. I cannot get rid of what I have become and must write my technical account accordingly. The alternative is not to write it at all.

1900 - 1908

Although I had drawn pictures of one sort or another from earliest childhood, the first actual instruction I remember receiving was at the Corcoran Gallery in Washington, D.C., when my father was in Congress. Saturday morning classes for young people were conducted there.

I was not much inspired, because we drew from wooden cubes and other geometric figures, the very appearance of which was forbidding.

I preferred as models for my picture-making the engravings in my father's history books, especially those which showed bloody looking battles. Earlier sources of inspiration were the famous barroom prints of "Custer's Last Stand" and the blowing up of the Battleship Maine, of which I concocted many versions. I never copied anything very closely, but let my imagination run freely when I redid a picture.

Some interest in painting was aroused by the exhibits at the Corcoran, but more by the historical paintings in the Rotunda of the Capitol and the murals on legendary subjects in the Library of Congress. I had no desire, however, to try my own hand at painting. My chief technical interest was in pen-and-ink drawing, which I modelled after the crosshatching style of the cartoonist Berryman, of the Washington *Post*. I became quite proficient at this—enough so, when I was seventeen, to hold down a job as cartoonist for the Joplin *American*, a newspaper in the bustling lead and zinc center of Joplin, Missouri. My success there set me to thinking of journalistic art as a permanent pursuit.

In order to improve my drawing for such a career, I enrolled in February of 1907 at the Chicago Art Institute. Shortly after my arrival there, however, my ideas of the future began to change. A very sympathetic teacher, Fredrick Oswald, in one of whose classes I had enrolled, induced me to try painting in watercolor. Under his guidance I made my first attempts at working directly from life with color. The experience proved fascinating and soon so engrossed my attention that I forgot my journalistic ambitions.

In *An Artist in America* I said that I took no training while at the Chicago Art Institute. I should have said that I took little of the usual academic training. Drawing from casts of Greek and Roman sculptures, which was the approved way of beginning such training, bored me. I did not have enough artistic background to understand these reproductions and did not like the niggling charcoal techniques used in copying them. Nevertheless I did well enough to get myself promoted into the life classes, and working in these at least half of every day, I acquired some knowledge of the human figure.

I obtained also in Chicago my first insights into the art of designing—of consciously planning, or composing, pictures before attempting to execute them. Japanese prints were, very largely because of James McNeill Whistler's influence, much in favor at this time. Fredrick Oswald, my favorite teacher at the Institute, was enthusiastic about these and encouraged continuous study of the way they were put together. Through continued observation of the prints I learned to arrange my pictures in definite patterns and acquired a taste, from such artists as Hokusai, for flowing lines which lasted all my life.

With Oswald pointing the way, I also improved my pen-and-ink techniques by copying the drawings of Daniel Vierge, a Spanish illustrator much admired in the early part of the century. I got rid of the constant crosshatching of the journalistic styles which had heretofore been my models.

1908 - 1912

While continuing to study watercolor painting and composition under Oswald, I also undertook oil painting, first in the class of a kindly and complaisant elderly artist named Freer and then in the classes of Louis Betts, a fashionable portrait painter of the time. Betts was a brush-work virtuoso who followed Sargent, Chase, and others of that school. I was not "officially" enrolled in the classes of these oil painters, but with the easy discipline of the Chicago Art Institute, I simply moved in. Both Freer and Betts favored a limited palette, at least for beginners. Since I was to come back to this palette—or one close to it—time after time in my later painting, it had better be described. It was composed of white and black, yellow ochre, burnt sienna, a Venetian red, and a green oxide dulled with black. Occasionally a blue might be added.

This limited range of color encouraged free brush drawing which, particularly with Betts, was essential to "vital" painting. The chief models for study in Betts' classes were Frans Hals and Velazquez, enlarged reproductions of whose works were tacked up about the classroom walls.

I did not do as well with oil paint as with water color, being unable to maintain any kind of drawing with the slippery, buttery medium. However, squeezing out the fat tubes of paint was fascinating, and I did finally discover some of their properties and was able to put that knowledge to use in the spring and summer of 1908 with landscape painting.

In spite of my experiences with other teachers, the chief influence of my Chicago studies remained that of Fredrick Oswald. Oswald later spent many years in Italy where little by little his eyesight failed. The last I heard of him he had returned to Chicago, totally blind.

With Oswald's encouragement and through the influence of a letter which he wrote to my parents, I went to Paris, France, in mid-August of 1908, enrolling a little later for the autumn term at the Académie Julian.

The Académie Julian vied with the École des Beaux-Arts for supremacy as the top art school of the world. It was famous everywhere as a factory for turning out draughtsmen. Since its methods and the ideas which propelled them have lost favor in our modern world and are dying out, it is necessary to describe them in order to explain how they affected me.

Training procedures at the Académie were not different from those I had encountered in Chicago, but were more rigorously applied and enforced. The figure-drawing classrooms were large and lit by skylights. At one end of each was a model stand, and radiating in a semicircle from that, stools and easels were set in such a way that all students could see the model, though those in the rear usually had to stand to do so. The seats nearest the model were reserved for the more advanced students who, while they were closer to their subjects, had problems of acute foreshortening to deal with. These "master draughtsmen" took pride in handling such problems and often would remain in the Académie year after year for the pleasure they took in solving them. For some of these students this kind of exercise became the "all in all" of art. They became perpetual students and never did anything else.

On each easel in the classroom was a drawing board to which was thumbtacked a lightly grained sheet of drawing paper. Each sheet on each board was the same size. The students drew with thin sticks of charcoal and always held erasers for corrections. Each and every one kept a plumb line handy, which was held up now and then to determine the correct angles of things, the angles which, for instance, the model's shoulders or hips took, in the perspectives resulting from the student's particular position. In working out these angles, it was the practice to close one eye to establish a fixed point of vision—an exact point of focus— somewhat as a camera does.

The whole method was strictly visualistic, and in a most narrow and rigid sense. But it had a philosophy. This went about as follows. Drawing and painting were visual arts. In order to make sure that you visualized correctly you were supposed to divest your visual experiences of all the conditioning effects of non-visual experiences. Such experiences distorted your visual ones. They made you see incorrectly. You were to get rid of your memory, your imagination, and all preconceptions they might engender and learn to see "purely," with what John Ruskin and the American philosopher William James called an "innocent eye."

This philosophy and especially the methods to implement it could be theoretically justified by reference to Leonardo da Vinci's famous "Treatise on the Art of Painting." But only theoretically, because Leonardo did not follow such methods in his own drawing.

I did not, of course, know at this time about the thinking behind the Académie's methods, but I could see their results. As meager as was my information about art, I was certain that such methods would not lead to any kind of art that I wanted to produce. I was not sympathetic to the charcoal techniques insisted upon in the drawing classes, as I have said. My habitual approach to drawing, developed perhaps by my constant use of pen and ink, put more emphasis on line than these techniques permitted. The poses of the models were held for a week, sometimes two, and it was hard for me to sustain interest for so long a time. To add to my general dissatisfaction with the Académie, my pride was assaulted when I was assigned for my first two weeks to a cast-drawing class. Nevertheless, I stuck to the place for eight months.

About the only things that permanently impressed me were the weekly lectures on anatomy, which were graphically conducted with a living and, usually, muscular model on hand for comparison with the diagrammatic expositions of the anatomist. These lectures, unlike the visualistic copying of the regular drawing classes, provided a real body of knowledge—something which stuck in the mind.

I studied at the Académie in the mornings. In the afternoons I painted in my "studio" or made pen drawings in the streets and in the cafés. The life of the latter was of absorbing interest, as it still is, for most Americans. In the early winter of 1908-09, under the direction of John Thompson, an American painter a few years older than I, who later lived in Denver, Colorado, I began experimenting with Impressionist techniques. This brought on, for the first time, the use of a full-color palette with oil paint.

Though the Impressionists had not yet, in 1909, reached the Louvre, there was a permanent exhibit of their works at the Luxembourg Museum. Among these was Monet's "Gare St. Lazare" and Renoir's "Moulin de la Galette"—both high marks of Impressionism. The picture that most attracted me, however, was a sunlit scene of red tile roofs and backyard gardens by Pissarro. Perhaps because of the clear-cut exposition of method in this picture, I made myself an ardent disciple of Pissarro and tried to paint as nearly in his manner as I could. I began with still lifes, but when spring came, carried my experiments out to the parks and streets of Paris.

My attachment to Impressionism was manifested, however, for only half the day. In order to escape the distasteful charcoal drawing of the life classes at the Académie Julian, I enrolled for my second term there in a painting class where I worked with a limited palette similar to that which I had learned to use in Chicago, with emphasis on the light and dark "tonalities" preferred at the Académie. The chief influence in this class was Jean Paul Laurens, an old painter of somber French "histories" who had considerable status in Parisian academic circles. Laurens would walk around the classroom twice a week, but he never gave direct criticisms. These were provided by one of his disciples whose name I have forgotten.

Here I began to divide my interests between opposed and contradictory styles of painting, which would be continuous in my Parisian experience and which would occur again and again thereafter.

At the end of the spring term of 1909, I left the Académie Julian and took to drawing independently at the Académie Collarossi, a famous sketching studio of the Quartier Montparnasse. There was no instruction at the Collarossi studio, but a model was always there, and by coming early, one could get close enough to see. This had rarely been the case for me at Julian's, where studio positions were always assigned. Also, mature and even famous artists sketched at Collarossi's, providing more stimulating examples than the plodders at the Académie Julian.

Shortly before I decided to dispense with academic training I had met another American painter, John Carlock, who had been in Paris for a number of years. Carlock—a nephew of the famous Elbert Hubbard, the Roycrofter—was an erratic, somewhat inarticulate, but basically intelligent, artist, who had passed through an Impressionist phase similar to the one now engaging me and had become a disciple of Cézanne. What was more important for me, however, he had taken seriously Cézanne's directives toward Poussin and the restudy of Classical and Renaissance art. He had become a student of the fifteenth and sixteenth centuries, especially of the drawing of those times. It was Carlock's view that more knowledge of drawing could be obtained by studying in the Louvre than in the classes of the academies. It was largely because of his promptings that I left the Académie Julian.

Under Carlock's influence and guidance I began regular visits to the Louvre, sometimes daily, making rough pencil studies of the drawings, sculptures, and paintings there. This was continued all during my Parisian stay and provided an introduction to Classical, Medieval, and Renaissance art. Carlock enlisted as an ambulance driver during the latter part of the First World War and was killed in that service.

Though much under Carlock's influence as to the past, I did not attach myself to his Cézannesque leanings. Cézanne was beyond my comprehension. My painting continued to be Impressionistic, with occasional veerings toward the "tonal realism" of the academies, on the one hand, and toward that of Manet, Courbet, and even Carrière, on the other. Carrière conducted classes, but I did not attend any of them.

Some time in the spring of 1909, I was much affected by an exhibition of the work of the Spaniard Zuloaga, and I tried for a while to paint in his broad brushing manner. Zuloaga's art was too Spanish in subject matter, however, for me to imitate successfully. Nevertheless this diversion led to a vivid interest in Zuloaga's predecessors—the Spanish masters in the Louvre—and to my first curiosity about Goya and El Greco.

In the early summer of 1909 I visited Chartres and after surveying the cathedral, remained for two weeks in the environs, painting impressionistically "en plein air." Working there also was a young French artist, who kept looking through little squares of colored glass while he painted. This excited my curiosity, and though my French was still pretty thick for technical discussion, I managed to ask him about it. He explained that the tinted glass, because it took the color out of his subjects, helped him find "les valeurs," the "tonal" gradations in nature from light to dark.

On returning to Paris, I procured a number of pieces of different colored glass and for weeks went around the streets looking at everything and everybody though them. However, this apparent absurdity led not only to a better understanding of "les valeurs" and to attempts to sustain them in my painting, but also to a deeper appreciation of the formal patterns underlying the colors of nature, those substantial patterns which persist beneath all changes of appearance. In later years I discovered that Leonardo da Vinci also advocated studying the effects of colored glass on the appearances of Nature.

By the end of my first year in France, though I had not much improved my picture-making capacities, I had acquired a small fund of new knowledge. I had a working acquaintance with French grammar and was able to read and, in a rough way, to write the language. I spoke poorly, but due to the complaisance of the French people at that time, I could generally understand and make myself understood. I had also gained some idea of the vastness and variety of the history of art.

Besides John Thompson and John Carlock, I had met a few American artists that were studying or working in Paris. There were not as many in those pre-World War I days as were to come later, but around the tables of the Café Dôme small groups of Americans would congregate in the late afternoons. I met Abe Warshawsky, Leon Kroll, Jo Davidson, Lee Simonson, Arthur Lee, Richard Miller, and Leo Stein and came to a nodding acquaintance with a number of others.

All of these artists were older than I, and this age difference, even when it was only a few years, made a great difference in the matter of companionship. This was a time when the notion of "individual genius" was taking a strong hold of artists' minds. Even those who followed the formulae of the academies nursed beliefs in their personal "uniqueness," in some cases to an absurd degree. In this atmosphere of personal superiorities the talk of a younger artist, if listened to at all, received only a patronizing tolerance. Young "geniuses" were supposed to listen when the elder and more experienced ones were gabbing.

As I was, even at this early time, inclined to speculation and liked to talk about the ideas with which the Parisian world was continually assaulting me, I resented the attitudes of my older acquaintances. John Thompson was a good friend, but discussions about art, if carried beyond applicable techniques, bored him. John Carlock was too much a mentor for real companionship. He was willing to reveal his "genius" but not to have any of its tenets questioned. I needed a "genius" my own age with whom I could share experiences on a level of approximate equality.

This need was taken care of in the late autumn of 1909 when I met another American artist, Stanton Mc-Donald Wright, recently arrived from California. Wright was younger than I by a few months, but his talents, precociously developed, easily erased that small age difference. When I first met him, he was painting somewhat in the style of Robert Henri, the bold brushing of which fascinated so many young Americans at the time.

As I still had, along with my Impressionist leanings, periodic veerings toward this sort of painting, I was impressed with Wright's facility. Little by little we began trading studio visits, which finally resulted in a close association. This lasted not only during my Paris stay but was taken up later in New York, where it had significant bearings on my development.

The winter of 1909-10 was occupied by daily drawing at the Académie Collarossi, essays at portrait and figure painting (one self portrait still survives), and devoted readings in French literature. The studies in the Louvre, initiated by Carlock, were continued, but now largely in association with Wright.

During the early winter of 1910 I was strongly affected by an exhibition of the work of the Neo-Impressionist Paul Signac and began moving toward a Pointillist method. The adoption of Signac's Pointillism led also to the adoption of his spectral palette and to a wholly new attitude toward "les valeurs," which I came to regard not as aspects of the colors of nature, but as qualities of color itself. The light and dark—"tonal values of nature"—were discarded for a scheme of "color values" based on the intensities of colors in the spectral band.

Translated into paint, the warm, brilliant colors—through yellow to orange to vermilion—took the place of the light "values." The cold colors—from the bluish greens, on the one hand, and purple-violets, on the other, to the deeper blues—took the place of the dark "values." Various mixtures of greens held intermediary positions between light and dark. The "local" colors of natural objects, with this schematic palette, were only approximately depicted. The modelling of a red apple, for instance, could end up as a cluster of color spots ranging from yellow to red to green to blue. The local color of the apple—red—might barely survive. Nature was thus symbolically rather than realistically treated.

Today, when we have become habituated to the most farfetched kinds of symbolism, the symbolism of Neo-Impressionism seems quite conservative. But in 1910, though not of the most "advanced" sort, it had a decided flavor of radicalism. When I moved into Neo-Impressionism, it was an adventurous step.

Heretofore the colors I had used when painting, whether bright or somber, corresponded as nearly as possible to those I found in nature. Now, instead of trying to represent such appearances I sought for schematic color equivalents. The theory behind this held that because of the low intensity of the colors of paint as compared to those of objects under real light, it was impossible to represent *things as they were* by imitation of their true colors. *Sensation* producing equivalents of these colors must be *created* if their impacts were to be "truly" represented with paint.

The Impressionists, though they held somewhat similar theories, had never carried them very far into actual practice. Though local colors were split up into vibratory color contrasts, the Impressionists generally adhered to them—a red apple was a *red* apple, a yellow banana a *yellow* banana. Neo-Impressionism still clung to the depiction of natural scenes but the *process* of depiction was governed, as I have indicated, more by color theory than by the actual facts of vision. Here for the first time I got involved in abstract problems which could not be solved by reference to what I saw before me. In association with McDonald Wright, who had by this time turned completely toward coloristic painting, the Neo-Impressionist theories were, as spring came, tried out in the environs of Paris, mostly at the ancient park of St. Cloud.

It is hard to realize today the temper of the Parisian art world during the time of my stay there. I have mentioned the pride of genius which prevailed. Beyond that, a very considerable number of the members of that world cultivated highly "intellectualist" attitudes. This was so, irrespective of how meager might be the scholarship supporting them or how uncertain the manner of expressing them in art.

There were no movies, no radios or other inexpensive sources of entertainment, so the habit of reading was widespread—much more so than in student circles of today, where it is rare to find a young artist who has information beyond that provided by the "arty-critiky" columns of the current newspapers or weeklies. Neophyte artists devoured books and attended Saturday morning lectures at the Sorbonne. They concocted theories, sought historical justifications for these, and the studios and cafés rang with arguments. Few painters took their easels before nature without ideas to test or exploit. Though most of these were immature and half-baked, some even ludicrous, they arose from a genuine and lively spirit of inquiry. And they fed a constant urge toward new and novel experimentation.

In this atmosphere my play with Neo-Impressionism did not proceed uninterrupted. I had not carried my trials with it much beyond their first stages when new factors, tending to divide my interests again, were introduced by still more radical schools which rose to public attention. Salons and gallery exhibitions began to be held regularly, and they displayed the work of all the "ultramodern" experimenters, including that of the "Fauves" and the emerging cubists. Although I had been aware of the existence of this new painting, the impact caused by seeing so much of it all at once was upsetting. The emphasis on design and especially the very novel varieties of that, and the totally arbitrary use of color—or what appeared to be so—introduced me to a mass of unsuspected problems. Among these was the problem of Cézanne's art. Its obvious influence on so many of the "modernist" exhibits made a better acquaintance with it now seem imperative. Although, for more than a year, my friend Carlock had tried to engage my interest in Cézanne's painting, I had, until now, failed to respond.

The cubistic block-like way in which the Cézanne pictures were put together, with multitudinous planes of varying colors and with a minimum use of light and shade, chiaroscuro, was foreign to any kind of pictorial designing I had learned to understand.

Up to this time my own ways of putting pictures together—my "composition"—in so far as it was a conscious process, rested largely on what I had learned from Japanese prints, to which, as related, I was introduced in Chicago. I had avidly devoted myself to the collection of these prints after I arrived in Paris. Very good examples, sometimes fine ones, were then obtainable for very little money at the small book and pamphlet stands along the left bank of the river Seine. The walls of my studio were lined with these prints, and I never painted a still life without including one in the background. When I started to make a picture, I would draw the contours or silhouettes of the objects which constituted my subject, arranging them in flat patterns after the manner of the prints and where possible with the flowing or curving lines characteristic of so many of them.

Though my studies in the Louvre had made me aware of a different kind of designing, one which proceeded by arranging solid forms in three-dimensional perspectives, I continued to design my own pictures as silhouette patterns, even when I intended a "realistic" portrayal and "modelled" the objects depicted or developed them by chiaroscuro.

This method of composing served very well for my "tonal" painting, just as it had for Whistler's, and it was equally serviceable for Impressionist and Neo-Impressionist painting. But it would not do for experiments in the manner of Cézanne.

A considerable amount of writing about Cézanne was already circulating in 1910, and it was easy to get a sort of literary acquaintance with his work. Cézanne's dictums, maxims, and directives were in print. His conceptions of the color-form, where form was built with color planes, had been described and, as I soon found, could be understood by studying his paintings. But his conceptions of FORM in the overall sense—the total pictorial forms he aimed to create—were still in an obscure state of definition. Cézanne's own statement of his aims, "that one must learn to do Poussin over again in the terms of nature," seemed clear enough at first glance, but it soon brought up, for me, the question of how to do Poussin over again in any terms. The "nature" of Cézanne was obviously the "nature" of the Impressionist palette which was familiar enough. The problem was Poussin.

After a few weeks of groping about, I concluded the answer to that problem must be found with Poussin's predecessors. This sent me away from Cézanne and back again to the Louvre. As a result, I did not at this time carry my experiments with Cézanne's color-form methods very far.

Breaking objects up into different colors had not been too difficult with Impressionism or Neo-Impressionism, whose color divisions were small enough to maintain the shapes of the objects. But when these divisions were enlarged to the size of planes, I found it impossible to retain any drawing. Had I sustained my efforts in this direction,

I might have learned to do so; but I might also have slipped into those Cézannesque mannerisms which were to become such widespread and eventually tiresome features of so much modern painting. So in curtailing my explorations of Cézanne at this impressionable time of my life, I probably did myself a favor.

It was not only the difficulty of penetrating Cézanne's work, however, which halted continued investigations of it. There were other kinds of art calling for attention. The influence of Gauguin was almost as strong as that of Cézanne and almost directly opposite in its effects. Its orientalist patterns, now being reintroduced by Matisse, were at this time coming into much prominence. Both Gauguin's and Matisse's methods were more closely allied to my own ways of composing than were those of Cézanne, dealing as they did with silhouettes rather than volumes; but they were too far removed from that traditional realism of European painting, which the masterpieces of the Louvre had impressed on my mind as a fundamental desideratum for my own work.

Impressionism had brought new practices but was nevertheless a realistic art; Neo-Impressionism, though generally more symbolic, still aimed to express qualities of the visible world. Cézanne was also a realist, but differed from the Impressionists in that he tried to reinforce his "sensations" of reality by turning them into the solid architectonic and sculptural forms of the sixteenth and seventeenth centuries. Cézanne was more truly the European traditionalist than all the other artists affecting my 1910 world, but I was not ready yet to profit from his example. The chief structural influence of his methods had led to Cubism which was already at this time moving too far away from recognizable relations with visual reality to engage my interests for very long. I must note at this point that, in spite of his later fame, I never saw a single Van Gogh painting while I was in Paris. I don't think I even heard of his name.

The constant shifts of method caused by my explorations of the new painting had, by the summer of 1910, brought me to the attention of the gossips among the American contingent in the Quartier Montparnasse. Hints began to be thrown my way that I was wasting my time, that I had no convictions and was unfitted for the pursuit of art. I should go back to America, some said, and see what more profitable line I could take up.

Although I was very enthusiastic about my various experiments and always felt that each change would lead to my artistic salvation, I now began to realize that I had done little or nothing in the way of substantial production. I could point to no accomplishments. I had not even exhibited in a salon.

Finding myself in this situation, I determined to get away from Paris, forget all theories, return to painting directly from nature, and see if I could produce any finished pictures. With the assistance of a French artist from Tulle, in the Midi, whose acquaintance I had made, I found a place in a small mountain village near that city. This area was quite rugged and offered attractive scenery full of running streams and numerous waterfalls. Landscape "motifs" were everywhere. I remained there from mid-August until early November, and freed from all the pressures of Paris, I did the best work of my sojourn in France. Amalgamating the various methods I had learned and casting out the influences I did not find immediately useful, I managed to complete some dozen canvases. Although a few were broadly brushed, I used the Pointillist method of painting with small spots of color for most of them. However, I abandoned all schematic color treatment, trying to paint the colors and "tonal values" of nature as they appeared. One of these paintings, a chestnut tree "Contre Soleil," has survived. The rest were destroyed, along with my other Parisian experiments and, in fact, nearly all my youthful efforts, when our family home at Neosho, Missouri, burned to the ground in 1917.

When November arrived and it became too cold for outdoor painting, I returned to Paris, hung my new work about my studio, and prepared some little cards announcing an "atelier thé" for its exhibition. Some of these cards I delivered, the others I left on the counter at the Café Dôme, where my American and English acquaintances could see them. This effort at self-promotion proved a complete flop. Only three people came—John Thompson, who was my immediate neighbor; John Carlock, my mentor; and McDonald Wright. Since my three visitors, though friendly to me, thoroughly detested each other, the gathering was less than a success. Wright was the only one to show real interest.

The purpose of calling attention to my new paintings was partly to improve my reputation as a painter in the Quartier Montparnasse, but also to get expert advice from some of the older artists about selecting a couple of my efforts for the 1911 Spring Salon. A letter from my father, which had come during my absence from Paris, warned me that the money set aside for my education was dwindling and also asked for proof that I was accomplishing something. I had not heretofore thought of submitting pictures to the Salon juries, but I now decided that I had better do so. Acceptance in a Paris salon would indicate to my home-folks that I was getting somewhere. I put expensive frames on two of my new pictures and prepared to submit them to the Salon.

Shortly after my return to Paris from the Midi, I had commenced reading Hippolyte Taine's *Philosophie de l'Art*, a collection of lectures delivered at the École des Beaux-Arts some years before. Except for samplings of John Ruskin's works, this was the first philosophical treatise on the Arts I had ever read. It made a deep impression. Revealing the close ties of the older arts to specific social backgrounds and cultures, it made me question many ideas about art that I had heretofore taken for granted.

In the artistic milieus to which I had adapted myself, it was generally assumed that art had its own separate existence, its own special problems and disciplines, and that these bore only a chance and unimportant relation to time and place. This was the Whistlerian view, as it had been expounded to me in Chicago, and something similar to it was accepted by artists everywhere. The independence of art had never been questioned by any of my friends or teachers. Art was for, by, and of Art. I now know that the tendency to regard each work of art as "unique" and to treat it as having a wholly self-sufficient existence has stronger philosophical support than could have been given it by Whistler or other artists of the time. However, though I recognize a certain validity in the viewpoint and do, in fact, often "respond" to works of art purely for their color or structure, I still do not believe they can be separated from their social origins without ignoring the place of meaning in the creative act. Art is not only form but, especially in the case of a representational form, also an expression of the artist's humanistic thinking and feeling; and as he is conditioned to think and feel as a human being by the culture in which he lives, some knowledge of that culture is needed for complete comprehension of what he has to say. Pulling artifacts out of their contexts is like pulling any other kinds of facts out of theirs. Who can really *understand* a Madonna painting without some familiarity with the Catholic cult of Mary?

The pictorial monographs about the various masters of painting, which I had begun to collect when I started my studies at the Louvre, should have brought questions to my mind about the relations of these different artists to their differing societies. However, it was not until I read Taine's somewhat florid but documented descriptions of the worlds in which these artists flourished that I began to think of such relations.

Years later the trends of thought germinated here would mature in an Americanist environmentalism, but for the moment their chief effect, besides making me question my own beliefs, was to bring up doubts about the directions being taken by the new Parisian painting—directions which were obviously moving it further and further away from any recognizable representation of either nature or society. Seen through Taine's writing, the art of Paris appeared to be feeding wholly upon itself; paintings were growing out of paintings rather than out of any discernible cultural situations. Though, as Taine seemed to spell it out, this was degeneration, the literature circulating about the new movements gave them a persuasive aura of "progressiveness" which it was difficult for a young artist to ignore. Even without Taine I would, at this time, have faced a dilemma.

Weighing my situation, it seemed to me that I must make a choice. Either I would paint in the realistic traditions of Western art with some kind of identification with the natural world, and thus risk being "unprogressive," or I would follow the new movements toward an unknown goal, a goal which a number of farsighted critics were already saying might turn out to be an empty square of paint.

Since I was unable to make decisions about the directions I should pursue, the opening months of 1911 were sterile and unproductive. They ended in almost complete discouragement. This increased when the jury of the Spring Salon rejected my entries and further increased with the knowledge that my Parisian sojourn was approaching its end.

At this time my mother, with my two younger sisters, arrived suddenly in Paris to see the sights of the city, putting me to some hot and fast scurrying around to disguise my way of life which, though conventional enough for the Quartier Montparnasse, would have seemed odd from a Missouri viewpoint. She brought the news that my father was unwilling to further support my Parisian studies and that I must either find a way to make a living in Paris or return home. As I knew the chances of money making for an American in France were too slim to consider, I reconciled myself to the return. In late July of 1911 I went back to America, to my home town in Missouri, arriving there just under three years after I had left it.

In my lecture tours of the thirties when questions came up about my Parisian work, I would answer that I had first studied at the Académie Julian and then had painted as Impressionist and Neo-Impressionist, leaving the sense of a kind of orderly progression. Actually the pattern of my Parisian experience was a most illogical zig-zag. I was subjected to too many influences to hold any direct course. I was, in fact, much too young and much too impressionable to lay such a course. So I arrived at no stylistic convictions.

Looking back, I think that the best I got out of my stay in France was an introduction to art history, a love for French literature, and an ability to think in a language other than my own.

Though I took some pleasure in the familiar scenes of my boyhood and in the friends I refound when I returned home and was glad, in a way, to be released from the constant theorizing of the artistic circles of the Quartier Montparnasse, I was at the same time restless and very much disoriented. The Parisian art world, for all its disturbing pressures, had come to be the only one which existed for me. I could envisage no artistic future apart from it. Hippolyte Taine's environmentalist philosophy of art had had some effects on my thinking, but not enough to make me believe that the Missouri environment could generate much in the way of painting. Years were to pass before I could come to that belief. Nevertheless, a painter must paint, so shortly after settling myself at home, I set about making portraits. Having a knack for catching likenesses, I so impressed my father that he began to accept the idea I had not wholly wasted my time in France. The streaks and spots of color I brought back from there had, of course, struck him as wholly lunatic. This recovery of his confidence was very important because it would lead, in spite of financial difficulties which were beginning to plague him, to further efforts to help me.

1912 - 1916

In early January of 1912 I visited Kansas City, hoping to find employment as a teacher at the newly founded Art Institute there. One of my erstwhile Chicago friends, who was director of the Institute, encouraged this hope, but nothing came of it.

Returning home, I again took up my portrait exercises, painting anybody who would pose. (Portraits of myself and my father survive. They were hanging in his office when the aforementioned destruction of our home occurred.)

To facilitate drawing, I reverted at this time to the limited palette first acquired in Chicago. Perhaps because of this my paintings began to have some stylistic resemblance. It was the first time that I had ever maintained one general painting direction for an appreciable period, in this case about five months. From the nature of the work—almost devoid of color and strictly realistic—no one would have suspected I had just spent three years amidst the coloristic explosions of Paris.

However, I was not yet ready to settle down. The flowering of a Missouri spring again brought an itch for color, and I did a number of landscapes with a full and high-keyed palette. As a Neo-Impressionist method was utterly inappropriate for the sharp contrasts and clear air of my Ozark subjects, I painted them broadly. I drew the objects depicted with blue lines and modelled with color within the defined areas, a method quite common in Paris which I had occasionally practiced while there. (One of these landscapes also escaped destruction and survives in good condition.)

With this springtime shift of method I again fell into those stylistic contradictions so characteristic of my Parisian experience, where my leanings shifted from a realistic, light and dark "tonal" painting, at one moment, to some kind of schematic colorism at another. This would continue to occur. It would be many years before I would be able to channel myself into a permanent way of painting.

Realizing that I would never make a living in my home town, my father agreed to finance a stay in New York, where I thought I might find opportunities with my portraits or with some of the commercial arts which flourished there. I arrived in New York in early June of 1912 and, as described in *An Artist in America*, set myself up in the old Lincoln Square Arcade, where some of my former Chicago friends were located. Here I met three young men who were to play important parts in my life. They were Thomas Craven, then teaching Latin in a private school, but later to develop into a highly controversial art critic; Rex Ingram, then practicing sculpture, but later to become a famous movie director; and Ralph Barton, then working for advertising firms, but soon to become one of the most successful of New York's magazine artists and, at a number of crucial moments, a "friend in need" for me.

Shortly after arriving in New York, I received a small commission to space the lettering and pictures of an importer's booklet on Japanese porcelain and china. Most of the wares advertised were used for decoration with vitrifiable colors, an art then practiced by women all over the country. Having a curiosity about techniques and wanting to know something about this one, I obtained an introduction to a Mrs. O'Hara, a lady then widely known as a professional china decorator. Mrs. O'Hara was a very conventional artist, but a skilled performer in her trade. Visiting her studio, I picked up the basic techniques for the application of vitrifiable paints and enamels, which I would later put to some practical use for myself.

I brought with me to New York several books of pen drawings I had made in Paris. I tramped about the city from one agency to another, showing these to people; but while some interest was aroused, it was not enough to produce any commissions. Perhaps if I had perservered, I might have found some kind of niche in the world of commercial art; but my thoughts were turned in other directions by a chance encounter with the New York painter Sam Halpert, just returned from Paris, who was later to become well known in New York art circles.

I had met Sam once or twice in the Montparnasse cafés, but the difference in our ages had then forbidden association. Now, however, as a fellow ex-Parisian, I was cordially received. Sam's somewhat decorative adaptations of Cézanne so strongly impressed me that I promptly forgot my commercial ambitions and went back to painting. Prompted by his urgings and encouragement, I began studying and copying the many detailed photographs of Cézanne's work which he had collected. Following his example, I began to break up my surfaces with gradated planes of color and came as near as I ever would to adopting a Cézannesque manner. (Some watercolors survive.)

My fascination with this Cézannism lasted most of the summer, but it began to lose force when I tried to use it with living models. Although I tended to veer about a great deal, the general "pull" of my painting interests went toward a greater concern with line and chiaroscuro than a Cézannesque style permitted. Though I continued to study Cézanne's designs, I ceased trying to inject the multitudinous color-plane divisions of his painting into my own. This was one aspect of his work to which I could never quite accommodate myself.

In the autumn, what appeared to be an alarming illness of my mother called me back to Missouri. Though she recovered shortly after I reached home, I remained there some seven months, thereby missing New York's famous 1913 "Armory Show," the exhibition which so radically changed American painting. This 1912-13 stay at home would be my last. When I returned to New York in June, 1913, I would remain there for more than twenty-three years; and when I finally came back to live in Missouri, it would be at Kansas City.

I again settled myself in the Lincoln Square Arcade and took stock of my New York prospects. One of my Chicago friends, Jack (Rolfe) Armstrong, was now receiving very substantial sums for heads of pretty girls, executed in pastels, which he sold to magazines and calendar houses. Although my father had given me enough money to last for several months, if carefully rationed, I knew I must start a search for income. If I could find a pretty enough girl, I said to myself, there is no reason why I could not paint straight realistic portraits of her and sell them, as my friend Armstrong did. Acting on this assumption, I sought out and discovered an attractive model who was willing to pose for a share of the profits if I sold her picture. My first venture was successful. I sold my young lady's portrait for one hundred dollars to a weekly magazine. This, however, was to be my only success in the pretty-girl business. Though I tried for weeks, I could not duplicate it. There was a formula for this kind of art which I was not able to understand or activate. Concluding finally that my first success was purely accidental, I abandoned the hope of further ones along this line. I continued, however, to try my hand in other commercial directions, though with but very moderate success. In passing, I came to have a very considerable respect for the skills manifested in some of the obscure areas of the commercial field. I had given some time, for instance, to a study of the various kinds of lettering that had developed along with the historic representational arts and had, in my own estimation, become a fairly expert letterer. I soon found there were everywhere people ten times more knowledgeable than I in this field and much more skilled in putting their knowledge into practice. The same was true with pen-and-ink drawings where reproductions had to be reduced in scale. Some of the techniques used in the drawings of objects for advertising catalogues were way beyond my capacities in spite of the fact that I had practiced pen drawing most of my life.

The Armory exhibition of 1913 had developed enough interest in Parisian art that magazines and books about it were now being widely circulated in New York studios. Reproductions of some of Braque's experiments that came to my attention induced me to paint a series of flat, decorative still lifes in muted colors. Not having any money to buy flowers, I abstracted them from a seed catalogue, stylizing them in decorative patterns. Though far from being commercially intended, this work brought me a commercial opening. I received a commission to execute five large floral panels for a Coney Island dancing pavilion. I netted thirty-five dollars each for these. Compared with the lowest of art prices today, this seems nothing, but in 1913 it could be made to stretch quite a way.

Seeing the commercial possibilities of a decorative art and remembering what I had learned about the use of vitrifiable color from Mrs. O'Hara, I invested some of my newly earned money in porcelain bowls and china plates which I decorated in the flat manner of my florals. This proved to be a fairly profitable venture. I sold all of my products. I would continue this decorative ceramic work, off and on, for some years, always picking up a little money with it. (A number of these ceramics have survived.)

Purely decorative work, however, did not long satisfy me. I turned again to portraits and, among others, painted one of my younger sister, then a student at New York's Barnard College. I submitted this picture to the National Academy jury, but it was not accepted. However, at an exhibition of the Academy "refuses," it attracted attention and was reproduced in *Collier's*, then a nationally circulated magazine—my first widespread publicity.

1914 began as a discouraging year. Though I was pick-ing up small sums here and there, I sensed that I was getting nowhere. The field of professional portraiture was highly competitive and occupied by men much more skillful than I at making flattering images. It was becoming very evi-dent that my pen-and-ink drawing would never be suitable for the magazine and advertising business. I might have acquired a position as "lay out" man with some agency, but that would have meant routine office work with no time left for painting except perhaps as a Sunday diversion. My painting itself was shifting its directions even more than it had done in Paris.

Tendencies toward a straight visual realism, as in my portraits, conflicted with equally strong tendencies toward various kinds of coloristic painting. Whatever I did in any direction seemed to conflict with what was coming out of Paris, and this disturbed me, because Paris was still the source, to my mind, of all consequential artistic performances. It was obvious from the illustrated literature of Paris which came to my hands that I belonged to none of its "progressive" schools.

In this time of uneasiness, my old friend and Parisian associate McDonald Wright came to New York, a much-improved and matured young artist and co-founder, with ,another American painter—Morgan Russell—of a new coloristic school of painting which they called Synchromism. The Synchromists had already exhibited in Paris and Munich, and Wright was looking for a gallery to introduce their work to New York. This was difficult, because there were few galleries in the city at this time. However, a place was finally procured, and the Synchromist effort was put on display.

The first impression I received, all the pictures being large and crowded together, was like an explosion of rainbows. However, as an act of friendship I visited the show nearly every day and soon found myself interested. It did not take long to grasp the general idea behind the work. The Synchromists had extended and intensified Cézanne's color-form theories, in which form was seen as a derivative of the organization of color planes. They had intensified these planes by abandoning completely the usual colors of nature, replacing them with highly saturated spectral colors, and had extended them into an area of purely "abstract" form. What most captured my interest, however, was the Synchromists' use of Baroque rhythms, derived not from Cézanne's work, as was the case with most of the Parisian painters who had experimented with such rhythms, but from the more basic source of Michelangelo's sculptures. Through its use of these rhythms, Synchromism seemed to offer a more logical connection between the orderly form of the past and the coloristic tendencies of the present than any other of the Parisian schools. As that form had been permanently embedded in my mind during my studies in the Louvre and as I still retained the interest in spectral coloration which had been aroused by Neo-Impressionism, I could look more sympathetically at the Synchromist effort than most of the New York artists who came to see it. I could not accept the repudiation of all representational art, which was the core of Synchromist dogma, but its procedures were interesting enough to induce experimentation.

However, at the close of his exhibition, Wright returned to Paris; and as I had neglected to inquire about the particular color system on which the Synchromist painting was based, I soon abandoned experiments with it.

Due to the rather exaggerated claims made in the Synchromist "Manifesto," which was circulated at the exhibition, New York artists, by and large, ignored the truly logical aspects of the work and gave it little support. Some resentment was felt, especially by those who had had Parisian training, that two unknown Americans should have had the effrontery to set up a school in Paris in competition with their Parisian "superiors." A number of coloristic similarities between the Synchromist paintings and those of Orphism, a spectral school initiated by the French painter Robert Delaunay, led to accusations of plagiarism. Many Americans at this time were so slavishly imitating French painting that all deviations from it were regarded as being in "bad taste." However, enough curiosity was aroused for quite a number of artists to visit the exhibition, and I widened my circle of acquaintances in New York's artistic world. Heretofore, most of my associates had been my old Chicago friends, all of whose ambitions were directed toward the commercial arts. Now, little by little, I began to move in a painters' society.

The problem of how to live there, how to maintain myself there, was partially solved in the summer of 1914 by my friend Rex Ingram, who had abandoned his sculptural ambitions to become an associate director in the moving picture business. Rex procured employment for me to do research and draw up elevations for movie backgrounds and sets. As the movies of these days did not employ color, I made my set designs and backdrops in black and white. My conceptions were enlarged and sometimes modified by professional scene painters. Under Rex's sponsorship, moving picture work, in one form or another, would continue for several years providing a basic, if sporadic, income.

Observing the scene painters, I became interested in "distemper," or glue painting, and began experiments with that medium. The quick drying of the glue solutions, with which their pigments were saturated, permitted rapid overpainting and precise brush drawing, both of which struck me as highly advantageous. From this time on, I would continue to experiment with distemper painting. Later it would lead to the egg-tempera techniques which I used for my murals of the thirties.

About the time I discovered an affinity for distemper, my attention was drawn to reproductions of those essays in Baroque composition, based on Cézanne's bather pictures, which such Parisian artists as Picasso, Derain, and Othon Friesz had turned out. I had known of such exercises in 1911, before I left Paris, and had tentatively tried them out, while under the influence of Sam Halpert's Cézannism. Now, to practice my new medium, I started a series of these "bather conventions," groups of nudes standing or sitting under trees or by the water. Thinking only of composition, I did these without reference to living models and soon fell into the same stereotypes as had the above-named Parisian artists. Because of this, I eventually destroyed or painted over these pictures; but the multiple-figure composition, nude or clothed, would continue to engage my interests and eventually, in the form of historical subject pictures, become a permanent concern of my painting.

In addition to these compositional exercises I made several portraits in distemper, using young actors and actresses as models. All during my connection with the movies, I was able to find willing subjects, male and female, for my drawing and painting. A certain type of physical vanity, common in the performing world, drew these people to me. In this I was most fortunate, because I never could have found the money to pay for their services.

Some time during the winter of 1914-15 I met Dr. John Weischel, founder of the People's Art Guild, a burgeoning Socialist-oriented organization in which many "advanced" painters of New York were interested. The Guild held regular meetings, which I began attending, at Weischel's home in the Bronx. There, social as well as artistic questions were discussed; and this led to my first readings in Socialist and Communist literature. Weischel was a mathematics teacher by profession, but his general scholarship embraced most of the social and aesthetic thinking of the nineteenth century. He was also a Marxist scholar, though not a "party" Marxist. Basic to his thinking, in aesthetic areas, was the need for the regrounding of Art, the reinstitution of its social functions. As a preliminary move in this direction he envisaged an amalgamation of artistic interests with the social interests of the workers' organizations, the unions. This was pretty Utopian, but some of the theorizing behind it was persuasive enough to attract me.

Hippolyte Taine had already prepared me for the general thesis propounded by Weischel—that art should regain a more purposeful place in society. If the unions could help with that, I was ready to go along.

In the autumn of 1915 Stanton McDonald Wright again returned from Paris, which was now war bound, and a close association with him was renewed—with him and with his elder brother, Willard Huntington Wright, now turning, under Stanton's guidance, from a literary to an art critic. Willard and Stanton were hatching plans for another Synchromist exhibit, but they had concluded that this time it would be politic to have it in conjunction with a few other artists. Stanton, who was, as in our Paris days, disposed to forward my interests, indicated that if I could produce the pictures, I would be included in the exhibition. As I had not lost my curiosity, aroused the year before, about the Synchromist color system, I asked to have it revealed so that I might explore its possibilities for my own work. This system, invented by Tudor Hart, a Canadian scientist-painter residing in Paris, took the form of a spectral wheel so divided that triads of harmoniously related colors could be automatically determined. I was immediately taken by its complete rationality and with my usual enthusiasm for a new painting theory set about experimenting with it.

During the autumn of 1915, Willard Wright engaged the interests of Alfred Stieglitz, the famous photographer and promotor of "modern" art, John Weischel of the People's Art Guild, Robert Henri, then at the top of his influence, and some others, in his and Stanton's exhibition plans. These had now been enlarged to include most of the New York painters who had been involved in the "modernist" movements of Paris. The large and imposing Anderson Gallery was induced to lend space, and the exhibition date was set for the early spring of 1916. The name decided upon for the project was "The Forum Exhibition."

In the autumn and winter of 1915-16, I produced a batch of pictures using Hart's color system, though in a somewhat arbitrary way. Following the Synchromist practice of the time, I based the compositions of these pictures on Michelangelo's sculpture. However, as the multiple-figure composition was again occupying my thoughts, I selected Michelangelo's early relief the "Battle of the Centaurs," rather than a single figure, to serve as a model for my creations.

In speaking of the works of Michelangelo as "models," I do not mean they were in any way copied. Quite the opposite, they were studied, their formal structures analyzed, and then reconstructed, often in utterly different patterns. Nevertheless the Baroque rhythms characteristic of Michelangelo's work were retained, just as Cézanne, in his efforts to restate "nature" in the terms of Poussin, had often retained such rhythms.

As before told, I habitually designed my pictures by line and contour, even when I so modelled their forms that they appeared to be "in the round." During the process of analyzing "The Centaurs," I radically changed this procedure and began designing with volumes, with the projective and recessive forms of sculpture. The familiar directive of Cézanne toward "the cube, cone, and cylinder, seen in perspective" may have somewhat prepared me for this shift of method, but it took my experiences with Michelangelo's "Centaurs" to occasion it.

Rendering my sculpturesque compositions with the coloristic means of the Synchromists proved more difficult than I anticipated. Remembering my earlier failures with multiple-figure compositions, where I had depended wholly on my imagination, I now referred continuously to living models, drawing carefully the anatomy and the actions projected in my compositions. I soon discovered that I could not preserve this drawing if I split it up into a multitude of color planes, and thus I ran into much the same difficulties with the Synchromist ideas of color-form as I had earlier with those of Cézanne—really greater difficulties, because the intense spectral palette of the Synchromists produced effects on the forms in my compositions not dissimilar to the effects of an actual spectrum when it is cast prismatically onto the objects in a room. The effect was to break up the forms into disconcerting streaks and spots of rainbow light.

The Synchromists had solved such difficulties by eschewing representational form almost entirely, composing abstractly with bands of overlapping discs and color planes. Although I made some attempts along this line, producing a few completely "abstract" designs, I drew back from wholly abandoning representational form for a disembodied color form. So my Synchromist discipleship produced no Synchromies.

In the end I painted each of the figures in my Forum exhibition compositions with what amounted to a solid "local color"—red, orange, green, or yellow—just as I might have painted a red apple, an orange orange, a green pepper, or a yellow banana in a still life. The interstices between the figures—the recessive parts of my designs—were painted with blues, deep violets, and blue greens. The effect was colorful, but tended to flatten my pictures. The highly saturated spectral colors, causing sensations of nearly equal intensity, put their forms all on the same level. What was conceived as projective or recessive ended on the same plane.

However, though I was not satisfied and later destroyed these pictures, they brought me my first serious attention in the New York art world. I received considerable notice in the press and favorable comment from a number of artists. But there was also a negative side to my debut.

The selection of artists for the Forum exhibition had occasioned dissatisfactions. Artists who were not invited to participate felt their talents scorned. Some refused to participate because they did not like the company into which they were to be projected. A few among those who did participate looked down their noses at their fellow exhibitors. There were many artistic prides aroused and jostled. The exhibition had not even opened before it was bruited about that I had taken up the Synchromist palette only to get myself exhibited. It was known that the exhibition had been largely organized by Willard Wright who, it was said, had special interests in pushing Synchromism and giving it the appearance of a large school. In the views of the gossipers I had taken advantage of the opportunity offered by this to get myself into public attention. This was the first of a long series of petty accusations which my performances would cause.

There was, unhappily, just enough plausibility to this one to make it sting. I had not, in fact, ever publicly shown any Synchromist leanings before my displays in the Forum show. And to add to the plausibility, shortly after the exhibition was over, I made another of my multiplying changes of direction. I abandoned the Synchromist spectral palette and returned to a nearly monochromatic one.

Though, as I have indicated, I was at first fascinated with the logic of the Synchromist color system, it soon began to take a secondary place in my interests. The continued study of Michelangelo's sculptural structures, which soon was expanded to his paintings and to the works of his predecessors and rivals, led me away from the Synchromists' color-form to a restudy of form itself. By the time I had finished my pictures for the Forum exhibition, this study was occupying all of my attention, and I was again back in the fifteenth and sixteenth centuries where, as will be noticed, my various enthusiasms for novelties generally ended.

What now interested me was an expansion of my knowledge about setting up multiple-figure groups in voluminal and three-dimensional arrangements and their extension in the perspectives of an illusory picture space—a space of my own creation, but which would parallel the space of the actual world. I thought that this study could be undertaken best by getting rid of color problems for a while.

The summer and autumn of 1916 were therefore given over to compositional experiments in limited color based on various Classical and Renaissance paintings and sculptures. I did not make these for exhibition purposes, but in the winter of 1916-17 they were seen by Charles Daniel who offered to show a selection of them in his gallery. I do not remember the exact date, but the pictures were hung in early 1917 and though not well received by the critics, elicited some public interest. Three or four were sold and survive. The rest I eventually destroyed.

At this point something should be said of Charles Daniel. Daniel was an ex-saloonkeeper, or so it was said, whose sympathies were aroused by the plight of the young experimental artists in New York. The established galleries would not show their efforts, nor would the academies. There was no place where they could bid for public interest except at Alfred Stieglitz's small suite on lower Fifth Avenue, and that was largely limited to those artists in whom Stieglitz had a strong personal interest. This was especially true of American artists. Daniel conceived the idea of a gallery open to all people of talent, irrespective of whether or not he liked their works or their personalities. He established a place in midtown New York in 1916.

The Daniel Gallery became an open center for the exhibition of contemporary American experiments ranging from Ernest Lawson's Impressionism to the Dadaism of Man Ray and the "expressionism" of Marsden Hartley. Daniel never indulged in value judgments, but exhibited anything he thought had been sincerely undertaken.

I am quite sure that Charles Daniel never really liked anything I ever produced, but year after year he showed my pictures, singly or in "one man" exhibitions, never being disturbed by the criticisms he had to take for this. When he could, he sold things for me.

His place became, in spite of his own imperturbable aloofness from critical judgments, a hot house of artistic quarreling. The arty gossips would hang around the exhibitions, needling out comments from the various artists on their brother artists' productions, which, with proper exaggeration, would be redirected to the ears of those commented upon. Suspicions and enmities were built up by this petty tale-telling; but in spite of the divisions aroused, all the artists liked and felt a great debt to Daniel himself.

1917 - 1919

To be in easier reach of the movie studios, where Rex Ingram continued to provide bits of work, I moved in the early spring of 1917 to Fort Lee, New Jersey, just across the Hudson River from upper Manhattan. I set up a studio in an old house there. Other artists were in Fort Lee—Walt Kuhn, Arthur B. Davies, and "Pop" Hart among them—and I began seeing them occasionally.

The New York world of "progressive" artists was, at this time, divided into four pretty well-defined groups—the Alfred Stieglitz group, the John Weischel group, the Walt

Kuhn-Arthur B. Davies group, and the Robert Henri-George Bellows group. There was some overlapping of these groups.

During the winter of 1915-16, when the Forum show was under preparation, I associated with both the Weischel and Stieglitz groups. After the show had ended, though I kept in some contact with Stieglitz personally, I moved almost completely into Weischel's group, chiefly because his erudition and social outlook made his company more stimulating to me. Stieglitz was a devoted protagonist of some of the younger artists, but his interest in these was more narrowly "aesthetic" and much more tied, as I have said, to personalities than that of Weischel. He was also almost totally without historical background in his love of art. He had no interest whatever in those explorations into the field of Classical and Renaissance composition which I undertook after the Forum exhibition, considering them "academic." Weischel, with his intellectual respect for knowledge in general, took a more generous view. He purchased a couple of the drawings made for these experiments and persuaded some of his friends to do likewise.

The Walt Kuhn group at Fort Lee was nearer in general outlook to that of Alfred Stieglitz and had the same tendency to make art revolve about personalities. There were, nevertheless, strong divisions between the two groups. Kuhn, as one of the chief organizers of the 1913 Armory Exhibition of "modern" art, strongly resented the fact that he had not been included in the 1916 Forum exhibition. He considered himself, and quite rightly, more responsible than Alfred Stieglitz or Willard Wright for the introduction of the modern idioms to America and felt that he should not only have exhibited with the Forum group but should have been included in the selection committee. This resentment did not include me, but Kuhn's pretensions to leadership in the field of modern art, for which I did not feel he had the historical knowledge required, made me uncomfortable. Because of this, I attended only a few of his Fort Lee gatherings. However, I saw enough of "Pop" Hart to become fascinated with his highly descriptive water colors and to have my old Chicago interest in that medium re-aroused. When it became warm enough, I made a series of water colors along the Palisades of the Hudson, often in the company of Hart. Some of these survive.

The return to water color revived my interest in distemper painting, and I began a practice which was later to become habitual. This was to *underpaint* with distemper and *overpaint* with oil. The distemper, drying rapidly, permitted me to make up my mind about what I was going to do in a third of the time it took with oil and without the risk of muddied color. Later, egg-tempera would take the place of distemper, but the principles of such combinations of mediums, the use of which was commenced here, are the same.

Some time in the summer of 1917, John Weischel made connections between his People's Art Guild and the Chelsea Neighborhood Association of the midtown, West Side section of New York. A "people's" gallery was established by the association on Ninth Avenue, as an educational experiment in popular art-appreciation. Weischel offered me a position as director. The position called for keeping the gallery open on Sundays and on alternate afternoons and evenings of the week. In addition I was supposed to talk with and answer the questions of visitors and get pictures from artists to keep the exhibitions supplied. It paid fifty dollars a month.

As free-lance work was becoming more and more difficult to sustain in the movie business, due to the tighter organization of the companies and the unions, I accepted the offer. The sum paid did not compare with the seven dollars a day which was my movie average in a good period, but it was much more certain. I returned to New York and set up a studio in an unheated flat at Twenty-third and Seventh Avenue, directly above a saloon and within walking distance of my gallery. To augment my income during the winter of 1917-18, I taught drawing classes for adults in one of the Chelsea Neighborhood Public Schools. (There I first met Rita Piacenza, later to be my wife.)

During this period I took up sculpture, modelling a number of bas-reliefs and two life-sized heads. (One head survives in plaster.) I also experimented with "abstract" constructions made of wire, strips of wood, brightly colored paper, and cloth. These constructions were not set up permanently, as are so many similar ones today, but served only as motifs for painting. Studies of them were made from several sides. The purpose of this procedure was to provide references for the painting of "abstract" forms, something to work from, which might give such forms the same kind of "reality" obtainable in a still life or other paintings from nature. The practice of making such constructions lasted, off and on, until 1919, when another kind took their place. Most of the paintings along this line were made on paper, but a number survive. Occasionally I would revert here to the Synchromist spectral palette, but without following its schematic divisions and with a considerably reduced saturation of color.

America was by this time deep in the First World War, and ascertaining that I was eligible for the draft and might end up in the European trenches, I signed up for the Navy. My call to duty came in the early summer of 1918, and after various experiences, I found myself assigned as an architectural draughtsman to the Norfolk Naval Base. The head of my department, seeing I had no training for such work, put me to making freehand studies of installations and activities about the base. This was my first reportorial work, except for some drawing in the cafés of Paris, since my newspaper days in Joplin, Missouri, in 1906. The assignment turned out to be fascinating and because of some new attitudes it generated, was to have lasting effects.

During the ten years from 1908 to 1918 practically everything I turned out, even those portraits and landscapes made from life, reflected my reactions to painting, to the styles and methods of painting. I was by turn visual realist, Impressionist, Neo-Impressionist, Cézannist, Synchromist, Constructivist, or I zigzagged between these. My outlook was almost entirely processive. My figure compositions, for instance, were just compositions—arrangements of nude or draped figures, standing or sitting around doing nothing, not even looking at each other. It was not so much *what* I painted but *how* I did so that was the prime concern of these ten years. Now the situation was reversed. My architectural bosses of the Navy did not care *how* I did things but how accurately I *described* them. The subject became, rather suddenly, a very important factor. Airplanes, blimps, particular kinds of ships, coal loaders, dredges could not be merely "expressed," they had to be accurately defined, their characteristics distinctly shown. Along with my drawings, and often from them, I made a series of watercolors which, though less detailed and much freer in execution, were primarily descriptive. A selection of these was exhibited at the Daniel Galleries in New York during January, 1919. Because they were the only wartime pictures yet exhibited, they attracted attention. A number were sold and no doubt survive in different collections.

During the latter part of my sojourn in the Navy I had been permitted to live "off base" in a Norfolk lodging house. In the parlor there I had found an old-fashioned four-volume history of the United States by J. A. Spencer, written in the middle of the nineteenth century and plentifully illustrated with engravings in the various styles of the period. Having nothing to do at night, I read and reread this work and examined its illustrations with increasing interest. They reminded me that similar pictures had often promoted the amateurish efforts of my high school days, when history reading had been a favorite pursuit, and I began to ask myself questions. Why could not such subject pictures dealing with the meanings of American history possess aesthetically interesting properties, deliverable along with their meanings? History painting, religious or secular, had occupied a large place in the annals of art. Why not look into it again, I asked, and try to fill the contextual void of my own painting, give it some kind of meaning? These and similar questions piled up. Though unaware of it, I began here that fundamental change of mind which was soon to separate me wholly from my Parisian background and give a new and, this time, permanent direction to my painting.

Discharged from the Navy shortly after the exhibition of my water colors at the Daniel Galleries, I returned to New York and worked along the docks of the West Side river front, first as a longshoreman, then as a cooper. When I had saved enough money, I went back to painting.

Immediately after my return to New York, I had gone up to the Bronx to see John Weischel and try to re-engage myself with the activities of the People's Art Guild. I hoped that Weischel might find some employment for me with one or another of the Guild's connections. To my surprise I found that during my absence in the Navy the

Guild had disintegrated. The artists had, little by little, ceased coming to its meetings. As Weischel did not seem to care very much, I had the feeling that he also had lost interest in the Guild. Maybe he had come to realize that the union leaders were not going to give much of their attention to art.

Seeking some kind of artistic companionship, I then began revisiting Alfred Stieglitz' place at 291 Fifth Avenue. This also had changed—changed in atmosphere. There was no one there except Stieglitz himself when I made my first call. The old gang of talkative artists and aesthetic "hangers on" was absent. Stieglitz told me a long story of wartime woe. There was no interest in art. America would not support a living art. Even with the arrival of peace he saw little hope of building a responsive world in New York. Americans were too aesthetically insensitive.

I told him that I had attracted some attention with my watercolors of naval activities and asked if he had seen the exhibition of them at Daniel's Gallery. He had. But he had not liked them. Showing me a new group of John Marin's watercolors, he explained why. "This is painting," he said. "Your watercolors are only tinted drawings— colored outlines. Do you always have to guide your painting with a lot of hard rigid lines? Why don't you try to free yourself like Marin?"*

I did not like this, but Stieglitz was kindly about his criticism, more so than he had ever been with me, and I did not get angry. As a matter of fact there was an element of truth about what he said, and I recognized it. I kept going to see him. One day several weeks after my first visit and an exchange of letters between us, he showed me a group of pictures by Georgia O'Keeffe. Not knowing how deep his attachment to Miss O'Keeffe had become, I said, "Stieglitz, these pictures are nice in color, but they are even harder in their outlines than mine." Stieglitz promptly informed me that I was not artist enough to make criticisms of O'Keeffe. This put an end to my renewed association with him.

---

* The above conversational lines are "made up." Alfred Stieglitz never talked directly to the point but wove a web of discourse over, under, and around a subject. One of Stieglitz' actual conversational sentences would, Faulkner-like, run to two or three pages of print.

Nevertheless I reacted to his first advice. I began painting without preliminary drawing. As my experiences in the Navy had reinstituted a need for objective references while working, I began with still lifes but when Spring came, returned to my old landscape motifs along the Palisades of the Hudson river, near Fort Lee. Though I made free expressionistic renderings, most of the work resulting was too close to an Impressionistic visualism to suit me. It conflicted too much with my now deeply imbedded need for a solid compositional structure and the articulated design of the Renaissance.

The old problems of vision and form, visual reality and design, began to plague me more than ever; and I went back again to a study of the sixteenth century. One day in the early autumn, while reading an article on Tintoretto, I came across an account of his procedures in the creation of the famous "Last Supper" in the Venetian church Santa Maria della Salute.

For this complicated painting, Tintoretto had made a small sculpture to work out the positions of the figures and give them a logical and realistic light and shade. Examining reproductions of the painting and comparing it with other Tintorettos, I became aware that they all possessed a similar sculptural quality and a similar concentrated chiaroscuro. I concluded that they must all have been designed in a similar fashion, by some kind of preliminary sculpturing.

As the idea of trying my hand at historical painting had persisted, it occurred to me that a similar procedure might help me with such a project. Historical painting would again involve me in multiple-figure compositions with which, for all my many trials, I had never been able to completely satisfy myself. Since my analysis of "The Centaurs," at the time of my Synchromist effort, I had continued to compose in a voluminal fashion, thinking in terms of the three-dimensional projections and recessions of sculpture. I could produce schematically well-ordered three-dimensional designs, like those of the Renaissance painters I admired, but I could not give them the "feel" of reality obtainable in a still life or portrait where I had something "real" to refer to. They remained purely schematic. Perhaps, I now thought, by modelling my compositions sculpturally, as Tintoretto had done, I could supply the concrete references I appeared to need. The *actual* forms of sculptured figures, projected in a real, even though miniature, space, would possess the same tangibility as objects in the space of the natural world. They could thus serve somewhat as the abstract still-life constructions I had made earlier. As these had provided some reality for imaginary abstractions, so might more representational constructions provide reality for imaginary historical representations.

Already with some experience in clay-modelling, I began to experiment with a sort of dioramic sculpture in high relief. I did not, of course, know how Tintoretto himself had proceeded with this pictorially-directed sculpturing; but I had seen dioramic carvings in the cathedrals of France, and I had detailed photographs of the pictorial reliefs Ghiberti had made for the doors of the Baptistry in Florence. I decided to proceed along some such lines. The first sculptures I made were projected very deeply and were largely cubistic in their structure. I wanted to define clearly the directions and angles of the different planes, so that I could more readily represent them in a pictorial space. At first I had difficulty maintaining the kind of formal relations that could be transferred to a picture surface, and I made many experimental drawings from my sculptures to test these. Where a suite of forms proved pictorially impractical, I would do it over and then draw it again. Often a whole sketch book of more or less cubistic drawings would be made before I could finally make a sculpture take on the pictorial character aimed at. Some of these drawings have survived and have led to assumptions that I was at one time attached to the modern Parisian Cubists. This is not so. Modern Cubism broke up form, split it into facets, and finally became not cubic but flat. It destroyed the conditions necessary for the realistic or illusory representations I had in mind. The cubism of my 1919-20 drawings aimed at restoring such conditions. The only cubism it is related to is the sixteenth-century cubism of Erhard Schön and Luca Cambiaso, which also aimed at the representation of a realistic world—a world of human action in three-dimensional extensions.

I spent a number of months learning to make effective dioramic sculptures and to compose pictorially with clay and plastilene. Most of the autumn of 1919 and the early months of 1920 were devoted to experiments with this process. Little by little I learned to reduce the depth of my constructions and to better control the relations between their forms. They became less cubistic and more flowing. In the end I developed modelling techniques which allowed me to compose rapidly and to arrive at a product whose concrete spatial reality was transferable to my paintings. I now had a method with which I could give imaginative conceptions a substantive character.

With these new compositional procedures, stylistic changes began to occur in all of my work. In a short while my painting so completely changed its character that a veritable chasm came to exist between what I had done previous to the winter of 1919-20 and what I did afterward. I would make many changes in the future, but from this time on they would all possess a certain stylistic continuity, imposed by constantly thinking in terms of a three-dimensional sculptural process. This would eventually come to affect even my studies from real life. I would come to draw people and landscapes, even fruits and flowers, much like sculptural carvings.

Although I did not know it at this time, I was returning here to what appears to have been a commonly used studio practice in the fifteenth and sixteenth centuries, not only by Tintoretto, but by other painters who wished to give purely imaginative subjects a semblance of reality. The painted bas-relief was a common form of decoration; it took only an extension of this in high relief to make a simulacrum of the real world, one which would provide all the conditions under which we apprehend the forms of that world, but with more logical and controlled relations between them. As indicated above, such a method implies the intent to create a somewhat illusionary representation. Plainly that is what Tintoretto and his kind aimed at, and it is what I aimed at when I started to compose sculpturally.

People have frequently asked why I should have bothered myself with so complicated a technique as that outlined above, when I could simply have hauled an easel and a paint box before nature and "let fly." "If you wanted realism," they say, "wouldn't that have been the easiest way to obtain it?" The question is somewhat naive. There is no realism, in the sense they seem to suppose, which persists as a permanent factor in the experiences of painters. There are many kinds of realism. The Chinese or Japanese flower painter has a different one from the Flemish or Dutch flower painter. These artists *conceive* reality in different ways, though both obtain patent realities in their productions. What my questioners apparently refer to is our western realism developed in the nineteenth and twentieth centuries, which is different from both. They are thinking of the visual realism of the Impressionists, which *is* obtainable in the direct manner they suggest. But, again, this is only one aspect of reality, the immediate perceptive aspect. The reality that we, as full human beings, generally know and act upon is more complicated. It is not the reality of direct perception but that which such perception leads to. The associations attached thereto constitute what we call our *knowledge* of things; they are our ultimate *human* reality.

This secondary, or *derived*, reality is a construction of our minds. It takes some kind of a parallel construction to represent it. This is a fact anciently known to artists and adhered to by all great artistic styles until the rise of purely visualistic Impressionism. My kind of reality needed the special techniques I developed to find an appropriate representation. It was not obtainable simply by looking out the window.

The adoption of a sculptural method and the espousal of its illusionary implications would, of course, tend more and more to separate my paintings from those of the twentieth-century school of Paris and from those in America deriving therefrom. Because of that and of the early use of the method to represent a nationalist subject matter, it would arouse sharp animosities among artists and critics and catapult me into twenty-five years of controversy.

A survey of the biographies of artists who have become widely known for their creations seems to indicate three phases in their careers. The first is devoted to a search for method. In the second phase *the* method is developed and its formal and representational potentialities are explored. In the third, the developed method is applied to the expression of those human meanings that the artist's life and beliefs provide. The first two phases are primarily technical, the last largely communicative.

In the old days the first two phases were developed in the workshop of a master, to whom the young artist was apprenticed. As the training was precise and its directions predetermined, the first phase was of relatively short duration. Most artists finished it before they were twenty. The second phase, where the methods were developed, might take longer, but the records indicate that the talented artists got through it and were ready for the third phase of social communication when they were still very young in years. Raphael was a master painter at twenty-five. Leonardo excelled his teacher at an even earlier age, and Michelangelo was a truly finished sculptor at seventeen.

This rapid progression from the acquisition of a method to the expression of socially consequential meaning is apparently not possible today. This is because there are no accepted traditions with regard to methods and no widely accepted social meanings to apply them to. Today's young artist is assaulted with such a multiplicity of methods that he never has time to learn one before it is outmoded and another is forced on his attention. The multitudinous shifts of modern life greatly shorten the tenure of both meanings and methods.

Changes in the patterns of what men believed were so moderate in the lives of Michelangelo and Titian that the meanings they expressed in their youth were still valid when they died. Today the meanings of people in one generation are often barely comprehensible to those of the next, because the situations which produced them have changed so radically.

It took me eleven years to go through my first phase and dig a method out of the artistic jungles of my time. It would take some seven or eight more to explore the second phase and make it serviceable for expressing the meanings that my experiences in American life were to provide. And, before it was finished, the third phase, unhappily, would find most of the meanings, which it took so many years to formulate, disappearing with the dissolution of the world that generated them.

However, this is not as bad as it sounds. Ways of life and the meanings they generate have a certain cyclical character and keep reappearing in kindred forms. The arts which express them do likewise. The Baroqueism of the sixteenth and seventeenth centuries reappeared in the Romanticist Delacroix and again in the Post-Impressionist Cézanne and through the influence of the latter, spread through our modern world, eventually affecting even the wildest of our "abstract expressionists."

When it reveals life, art becomes a form of history— and of the most vivid kind. We revive and can relive the past through the reflections provided by its art. We know the actual life of mid-nineteenth-century France better by the pictures the painters and novelists made of it than by all other records. So art is not only art but a regenerative force and because of that, permanently valuable to men. Forgotten meanings may come again to life, and the dead artists who represented them live again.

During the winter of 1919-20, I tested my new methods with two large multiple-figure paintings. One of these—a sort of garden scene, with a group of people and a dog—was promptly purchased by well-to-do friends for an over-mantle mural. The other was my first essay at a muralistic historical painting. About a year later it was entered by the architect Ely Kahn in an Architectural League exhibition where, though an object of some controversy among the architects, it put me up as a potential muralist.

Because I was primarily interested in form, both paintings were executed with a limited and "low toned" palette. (Both paintings survive.)

1920 - 1930

In July, 1920, urged by my ex-Chelsea student and soon-to-be wife, Rita Piacenza, I went to Martha's Vineyard, following her and another young woman, who were on their vacations, to that then lonely island. There I met Boardman Robinson, who was preparing to leave a distinguished career as a newspaper cartoonist for adventures with painting. This was an important meeting for me. Robinson was to be a friend and helper year after year. We held kindred attitudes. We were both beginning to be much dissatisfied with the more and more esoteric tendencies of the schools of Paris and the influence they were exerting in the United States. We also shared a somewhat similar political outlook.

Robinson belonged to a small colony, just established in the Martha's Vineyard township of Chilmark, the members of which held what at the time were called "extreme liberalist" views—that is, they looked doubtfully on the future prospects of our capitalist societies, pondered social changes therein, and gazed with approving curiosity at the Marxist-oriented Russian Revolution. Robinson had been in Russia as a newspaper correspondent and was a close friend of John Reed, the famous American propagandist of the Russian Revolution. He was also close to the Socialist cartoonist Bob Minor, who was then working at organizing an American Communist party. He knew the Socialists Eugene Debs and Norman Thomas. He knew Roger Baldwin, Jerome Frank, Felix Frankfurter, Morris Ernst, and others who were then questioning American society in the postwar world. All of these men visited the Chilmark "liberalist" colony at one time or another; I met and talked with them and some became permanent friends. Readings that I had undertaken before at the suggestion of John Weischel, of the People's Art Guild, had prepared me somewhat for the thinking of Robinson and his group. Like Weischel, all in that group believed that the "modern" art growing in the postwar world was lacking in social value and unless it re-attained some of that value, it would soon fall into decadence. Although Radek's "social realism" had not yet found a foothold in artistic thought, similar, if less party-ridden, ideas were beginning to occur to thinking people everywhere.

All of this coincided with the non-political but equally societal views of art that I had extracted from Hippolyte Taine. Though Taine's actual writings had by now become somewhat overeffusive for me and seemed much less discerning than they had appeared earlier, the thoughts they had first generated kept growing and were making me more and more dissatisfied with all "art for art's sake" thinking, with all "purely aesthetic" attitudes. So I found myself in congenial company.

In 1920 the island of Martha's Vineyard was difficult of access. You came by boat from the old whaling town of New Bedford, three hours away on the mainland. To reach the Chilmark area of the Island you hired a Model-T car and bumped your way for eighteen miles over skimpily paved roads. Once arrived in Chilmark, you walked whenever you wanted to go anywhere, were it twenty yards or five miles. Commercial fishing was the main occupation of the native people, but small farming and sheep raising were also carried on. Like all people who live in near isolation for long periods of the year, the Chilmarkers were friendly, glad to talk and visit at the general store and at their homes. Finding willing models among them, I began in the summer of 1920 my first essays in American genre painting. I proceeded with this by making careful drawings from life, then modelling my compositions in clay, then tinting the clay figures with black and white paint to simulate differences of local tone. I painted my pictures with constant references to the drawings and to the clay models.

I continued this kind of Yankee subject painting year after year, for I would return to Martha's Vineyard from this time on. Quite a number of these paintings survive. Among them is the double portrait in the Whitney Museum in New York City, called "The Lord Is My Shepherd."

During the winters in New York City, I developed my history project. The plan for this had now been worked out as a progression of chapters, each chapter to contain five formally related pictures covering, over all, twenty-five feet of lateral space. The first chapter was to symbolize the period of discovery and settlement, the second the period of colonial expansion, and so on. The whole project was conceived as more symbolic than specifically factual. Having acquired Ely Kahn's support, I counted on the Architectural League to exhibit my history as I produced it.

Though the history project was uppermost in my mind, I found time for other things also. During the winter of 1920-21, I again executed two large figure paintings, based rather freely on our seashore life at Martha's Vineyard. Like my histories, they were generalized scenes. One of them was sold to a well-known New York lawyer of the time in whose home it became known as "Basketball in Hell." In the mid-1960's it came up at auction in the Parke-Bernet Galleries in New York and went to the famous Hirschorn collection, though under a less lurid title.

During this period my associates, besides Boardman Robinson and his friends, were Preston Dickinson, who had, like myself, experimented with Synchromism in 1916; William Yarrow and Arthur Carles, Philadelphia painters who frequented New York artistic circles; Thomas Craven, now becoming an established art critic; the musicians Charles Seeger, Carl Ruggles, and Edgar Varese. Most of these people met once or twice a week at the apartment of Tom and Sarah Kelly, wealthy Philadelphia emigrants to New York, who made a practice of wining and dining their indigent acquaintances of the art world. My old Parisian friend and associate McDonald Wright had, by this time, departed for his native California, where, having given up abstract Synchromism, he was painting a new kind of "Chinoiserie" which took form in spectral versions of Confucius, Laotse, the Buddha, and rainbow shining "Chinee" ladies in the nude.

In 1922 I was invited by my friend Arthur Carles to participate in an exhibition of American "moderns" at the old Pennsylvania Academy of Art in Philadelphia. This exhibition, somewhat like the Forum show of 1916, but with a larger complement of artists, brought my sculptural painting its first public acceptance. Carles, though himself more interested in coloristic expressionism than formal expression, gave my work strong support. Through his recommendations the three paintings I exhibited were sold to Philadelphia collectors. One of these, the second of the large seashore multiple-figure pieces, mentioned above, went to the Albert Barnes Foundation.

Albert Barnes was an irascible patent-medicine millionaire, who had made his fortune from a product called Argyrol, then thought to be indispensible for eye troubles. He had a genuine passion for art, and his purchases of Impressionist and Post-Impressionist paintings had made the Barnes Foundation collection the best of its kind in America. In addition to being a collector of paintings, Barnes was a student of psychology, the jargon of which he used for the composition of insulting letters to people he disagreed with. As he eventually found himself at odds with nearly everybody, he had become notorious for these letters.

I met Barnes and was, with Thomas Craven, who was then writing art reviews for *Dial* magazine, invited to his home. The visit went well and ended by Barnes suggesting that he bring the two of us every weekend from New York for discussion about his Foundation projects. He needed a writer, he said, for a book on painting, and he might also employ me. After a few visits, trying to clinch my employment, I brought some of the cubistic drawings I had made for my sculptures and told Barnes that similar diagrams might serve to explain the designs of many works of art. Barnes asked how I would handle the Impressionists with such drawings. I was impolitic enough to say that the Impressionists were not notable in matters of compositional form and that it would be useless to approach their work with that in mind. Barnes, who was then avidly collecting Impressionists, unfortunately took what I said to be a slur on the school, and a few days later wrote me one of his famous letters, which broke off all relations between us. He got rid of Craven at the same time.

While my successes at the Pennsylvania Academy Exhibition were substantial, providing more money than I had ever earned before, they did not continue. Collectors of art were few in these times and fewer still where the experiments of young American artists were concerned. However, I possessed a source of income, modest but quite dependable, which enabled me to keep painting.

While attending sessions of John Weischel's People's Art Guild, I had met Dr. Alfred Raabe, a physician practicing in the Bronx area of New York. Later, after several visits to his home, we became close friends. He purchased a couple of my paintings and several pieces of ceramic, decorated porcelain vases. After I came back from the Navy in 1919, my friendship with him was renewed.

Dr. Raabe had a hobby. In the basement of his home he did cabinet work and other forms of skilled carpentry. This provided relief from his medical practice. In the winter of 1919-20 he had begun framing small paintings, watercolors, and drawings which he found in my studio, experimental things which, except for his interest, I would probably have destroyed. These pictures he would hang in the houses of his patients, leaving them there until the people got used to them or until a spot would appear on the wallpaper when they were removed. Then he would sell them for small sums— twenty, twenty-five, or thirty dollars. During the early twenties these sales kept me going. Sometimes, to his wealthier patients he would sell larger pictures and extract larger sums. One year he made nearly three thousand dollars for me. The Bronx became filled with Bentons. I guess they are still there, because I have never heard of one of them being put up for sale—even after I got sort of famous and my paintings began to be worth more than pocket money.

In the winter of 1923-24, I finished the first chapter of my "History of America." The twenty-five feet of wall space needed for its display made it a difficult entry for the Architectural League. However, with the help of the architect Ely Kahn and muralists Fredrick Marsh and Putnam Brinley, it was accepted and hung there. It received a great deal of attention, including some sharp critical attention. Architects in general were then committed to the idea that mural paintings should not break the plane of the wall. They should be flat, pale in color, and unobtrusive. The French muralist Puvis de Chavannes provided the most acceptable type of mural. My "History" was totally at odds with this. It presented strong contrasts of light and dark, was agitated in its form and color, and was too projective and recessive to stay flat on the wall. A few architects defended it, but even the most favorably disposed doubted that I'd ever get a mural commission with such painting.

Among the "modernist" aesthetes like those of the Alfred Stieglitz group, the emphasis on subject matter, particularly on the kind which I had chosen—American History —was most skeptically received. This was the time, it must be remembered, when most "progressive" artists were minimizing the importance of any kind of subject matter. Evocative subject matter, such as that of my "History," which suggested meanings beyond painting itself, was particularly frowned upon. Storytelling subjects were for book illustrators, not painters. Although I had, at times, gone along with such views, continued studies of the history of art, particularly of fifteenth- and sixteenth-century painting, had, by now, radically changed my mind. I had come to believe that meanings had a generative function. I concluded that the forms of a Giotto, for instance, resulted quite as much from the meanings that inspired him as from his technical discoveries or his observations of nature. As I now saw it, his religious stories had a constructive as well as a communicative place in his art. Form was, therefore, to a much greater degree than our modern artists realized, a "function" of the subject.

I had discussed such ideas with a number of people— Alfred Stieglitz, Boardman Robinson, Thomas Craven, John Weischel, even Albert Barnes, and others—and had jotted down a lot of notes about them. In the winter of '23-'24, I put these together in the form of an article and showed it to Forbes Watson, who was editor of *The Arts*, the chief art journal then circulating in America. Watson was favorably disposed and published it, thus adding to the atmosphere of controversy that was beginning to build up about my work and ideas, a controversy in which Watson himself would later take bitter sides against me.

During this time, as a diversion from my imaginative history compositions, I began making drawings and water-colors of New York street life, concentrating particularly on building activities, of which there were a great many. More and more the immediate scene began to fascinate me, as it had done at the Norfolk Naval Base. Also I had in mind the future need of such material for my "History," which, as I envisaged it, would some day encompass the twentieth century.

In March of 1924, I returned to Missouri to watch over my father, who was dying of cancer in a Springfield, Missouri, hospital. Springfield was in Ozark hill country similar to that of my home town, and its familiar character gave me a nostalgic feeling. The people who came to see my father also affected me by their frank, outgoing friend-liness. I made up my mind to see more of them and to re-gain touch with their country which, I reflected, was also mine. I guess I began at this time my return to Missouri, though it would be another eleven years before that was accomplished in fact.

During the winters of 1925 and 1926, I completed the second chapter of my American history, which was also exhibited at the Architectural League. During this time, having come across Cennini's famous treatise on Renais-sance techniques, I started working with the tricky problems of egg-tempera painting. I also returned to experimenting again with distemper. To get richer color for the latter, I made the mistake of using too heavy a glue solution, with the consequence that most of the paintings cracked so badly they were not worth preserving.

My histories had by now given me something of a reputation as a mural painter, with some people an acceptable reputation. A group of well-wishers began to seek commissions for me. There were four large spaces in the New York Public Library at Forty-Second Street and Fifth Avenue which were eminently suitable for paintings. It was suggested that I make designs for these, representing stages in the history of New York City, which could be submitted to the Library officials. If they were accepted, my friends would raise by subscription the money needed to execute them on the large scale required by the Library walls. Therefore I made four paintings, six feet high and a little over three wide, for this project. The work attracted attention, *The New York Times* giving it a full rotogravure page, but somehow it was impossible to get like attention for it at the Library. So the project faded away.

Shortly after this I received a commission to make four decorative panels for a sportsman's den, which brought in enough money to make possible another visit to Missouri. I arrived there in early May and took a three week walking trip through the Ozark Hills of southern Missouri and northern Arkansas, making pen-and-wash drawings as I went. This was the beginning of those studies of the American rural scene which would hold so much of my interest for the next fifteen years. It was the beginning of what came to be called my "Regionalism."

A selection of the drawings and of the watercolors made from them were shown in the winter of 1926-27 at the Daniel Galleries in New York. A written account of my Ozark adventures, accompanied by some of my drawings, was later published in *Travel*, a magazine put out by the McBride Publishing Company of New York. This led, some years later, to my writing *An Artist in America* for that company.

After completing my Ozark hike, I went out to the West Texas oil country, then "on the boom." I made many drawings of the western oil industry and the rough life accompanying it. One of these, a street scene in the then wild town of Borger, became the subject of one of my best-known "Regionalist" pictures, "Boomtown."

I carried my explorations on this trip as far west as Santa Fe and Taos, returning east at the end of the summer. In the autumn Boardman Robinson put out a strong hand at the Art Students League in New York and procured a teaching position for me there. I taught at the school for nine years, until I returned to Missouri for good.

By the middle twenties I began consolidating the second phase of my development. My life and work commenced taking on very definite patterns. In the winter I would teach and paint in New York, with occasional sessions at some of the Eastern colleges, Dartmouth and Bryn Mawr among them. In the summer I would be for the most part at Martha's Vineyard, where married by now, my wife and I were acquiring properties. Every year in the spring or early autumn I would take a trip for several weeks into the hinterlands, generally into some mountainous country of the South—Virginia, North Carolina, east-Tennessee— or westward into the Missouri Ozarks.

These were inexpensive trips, as they had to be for me. They began by train or bus, to get out of heavily settled areas, and were continued, mostly, by foot, with occasional rides picked up in some friendly fellow's Model T. I slept in small country-town hotels, many times in the homes of new friends with whom chance had made me acquainted, and sometimes on the ground. I travelled with a knapsack on my back, in which I carried a heavy Navy jacket, a few changes of light clothes, and sketching materials. On each trip I made quantities of drawings. These also began to take on a definite pattern. Having in mind their possible use for painting, I treated these drawings somewhat as maps of form. I avoided any close representation of naturalistic lights and shadows, trying to reveal only the basic anatomy of things, so that I could treat them later with any kind of light and shade I desired. They were, in this respect, somewhat like sculptor's drawings, though generally suggestive of more spatial extension. Most could be readily turned into sculptural forms, projected in clay or plastilene.

Sometimes I would make two drawings of the same subject; one to find its general form, another to describe the detail of that form. The work was exploratory and reportorial and at no time intentionally "aesthetic." I was not trying to make exhibition drawings, only useful ones. I learned to produce them with great rapidity, and I often ended a trip with three or four filled sketch books. Not every drawing was successful, nor was this important, for the very making of it would cut a memory impression and thus help build up the general image of America which I was now searching for.

I developed a constantly repeated formula for this field reporting. After the first few days of my 1926 walking trip through the Ozark hills, I noticed that the drawings in my sketch books, which were made with pencil, were beginning to smear. Due to the movements of my walking, the pages of these books were rubbing together, sometimes almost obliterating the drawings. I began, then, a practice of covering the main lines of these with India ink and washing a thin tone of watercolor—sepia or umber—over the rest. The gum in the watercolor held the pencilled modellings. In this way I was able to preserve my material intact for later use.

All of this poking around the country was not, however, "for art's sake" alone. It was also "for fun" and, to no small degree, for release from art, or from the world of art. This world is not only one of genuine talents and real creative energies but, in our times, where the artist has such an ambiguous relation to society and must base his claims to status so much on his own personal uniqueness, it is also a touchy one of easily-hurt prides. Each artist nurses and broods on his own particular genius, and any slip of the tongue, which might remotely appear to question that, creates an uneasy situation. Although I was committed to this world, was a part of it, and inescapably involved in its pathology, I nevertheless felt, at certain times, a pressing need to get away and forget it.

I do not mean to propose here the old Philistine opinion, so prevalent in my youth, that the artistic world is made up of "nuts." Far from it. In my long experience with that world, I have seen some odd behavior, and have also myself engaged in some, but I have met no real candidates for the bughouse. I have known only one full-fledged alcoholic and only two paranoids whose cases were noticeable. There are but few artists on record with really serious mental disturbances.

The artist of our times does suffer from an unhealthy social isolation that breeds, as I've said, a somewhat abnormal self-concern, but this latter is generally sporadic and is absorbed most of the time by his greater concern with his work. What I fled from was not the psychic troubles of artists but the overspecialized and narrow world to which modern circumstance had confined their activities.

Once in a while I would find a companion for my travels, a younger student friend who liked me for myself rather than for what he might learn from me. One of these was Bill Hayden. Bill went on several trips with me. The first, which is described in *An Artist in America*, was in the summer and autumn of 1928. We started out from New York in a station wagon, equipped for camping, and toured the southern mountains, the cotton and rice and sugar country of the Deep South, and the western cattle country and the Rockies. A mass of drawings came of this expedition, and a selection from them was shown at the Delphic Gallery in New York in December of 1928.

The Delphic Gallery was founded by Alma Reed who, as a buxom and attractive blond reporter for some press organization, had found herself in Mexico at the time of the first successes of the Mexican School of Painters. Alma envisaged a resuscitation of the Greek mysteries of Delphi in a new and modern form. This was considerably too esoteric for me, but because Alma had the Mexican painter Clemente Orozco in tow and because I had a great admiration for his work, I joined her organization.

I had looked with much interest on the rise of the Mexican school during the mid-twenties. In spite of the Marxist dogmas, to the propagation of which so much of its work was devoted, I saw in the Mexican effort a profound and much-needed redirection of art towards its ancient humanistic functions. The Mexican concern with publicly significant meanings and with the pageant of Mexican national life corresponded perfectly with what I had in mind for art in the United States. I also looked with envy on the opportunities given Mexican painters for public mural work. After I had completed the second chapter of my history, I began to question the practical side of continuing it without similar opportunities. I saw that I would soon have more large pictures than I could take care of. I must find walls, I decided, or give up the idea of my mural history. As Alma was also hunting mural space in order to introduce Orozco to New York, this subject of walls was continually discussed among the three of us. The problem, as I saw it, was not only to find the walls, but patrons willing to pay for what we put on them. It was Alma's view that it would be necessary to do the first murals for little or no compensation, in order to win the approval of architects. I could not agree with this, feeling that what was done for nothing would be regarded as worth nothing. I had been painting muralistic canvases for the Architectural League exhibitions for seven years, and they had so far got me nothing but a controversial reputation which was not worth a dime. However, as it turned out, Alma was right.

At this time Alvin Johnson, founder of the New School for Social Research, had raised enough money for the erection of a building for the school on West Twelfth Street near Fifth Avenue. Hearing of this, Alma visited Johnson and offered Orozco's services as a muralist. They were accepted. Orozco would paint a mural for the New School's dining room for the expenses of execution.

Alma did not inform me of this arrangement, but I heard of it from Ralph Pierson, a writer, teacher, and lecturer about art, well known in New York art circles. Pierson, one of the few critics who supported my Architecural League experiments, said he was going to make a protest to Johnson. He said it was outrageous that I who had worked so long at developing a new mural style for the United States should be ignored on this important muralistic occasion. Pierson made his protest, and Johnson replied that he had room for me, too, if I would work on the same terms as Orozco.

Later, at some Greenwich Village gathering, Lewis Mumford, another supporter of my Architectural League efforts, introduced Rita, my wife, to Johnson. Rita, by now aware of the whole situation, promptly offered my services to him. Johnson, who knew of my American history projects and who was delighted with the prospect of another mural, said a fine painting space was provided by the New School's Board Room. So I found my first public wall.

Unfortunately the news of this was received very frigidly by Alma, who felt that I had taken advantage of the opportunity she had found for Orozco to provide one for myself. This, of course, is precisely what occurred, but I felt that as a member of the Delphic team, some consideration should have been given to my interests. The discussions of mural prospects, noted above, had always included myself as well as Orozco. I was, therefore, shocked when Alma took my entrance into the New School projects as an opportunistic intrusion. But that is the way it seemed to her; and as she found among a number of artists a receptive audience for her views, I was again saddled with the title of opportunist. And again the title was plausible.

I must add here that this situation did not affect my relations with Clemente Orozco. We always remained on friendly terms.

By this time my explorations of American life were providing the subjects for all my easel paintings; and I decided that instead of referring to past history, as I had done for my Architectural League work, I would make a survey of contemporary America for the New School mural. I had all the subject material necessary in the drawings of my sketch books, and after getting Alvin Johnson's approval of the project, I set about organizing it.

The representation of such a theme would necessitate the amalgamation of many subjects having little or no relationship to one another, certainly no pictorial relationship. The problem was to get them together in such a way that they would function as parts of an overall pictorial form. This was solved by composing each subject unit so that some parts on the periphery of its design were left open. Or, to put it another way, some forms on the edges of each pictorial unit were so arranged that they could be connected with the forms on the edge of the adjoining units— locked into them, that is. The bas-reliefs of Hellenistic, Etruscan, and Roman sarcophagi provide many examples of such interlocking of formal units; so there were precedents to which I could refer. The difference between these and the units of the New School mural was that each unit in the latter was contextually different and often completely different in form as well. Units, for example, representing industrial complexes differed wholly from those showing agricultural scenes. In some areas of the mural where these differences were so great that peripheral jointures were too difficult to make, sections of the moulding that framed the mural were injected into the mural design itself. Separations such as this are often found in the illustrated pages of nineteenth-century magazines and books. When pictures had different meanings, it was then a common practice to separate them by decorative linear patterns. I followed this in the New School mural. Obvious as its purpose seems, this simple device has brought me more questions than anything in the whole painting.

The mural was done on panels of wallboard, reinforced with one by three inch cradling. A heavy linen was glued to the panels and coated with gesso (glue water and whiting). Work began with underpaintings of distemper and was finished with overpaintings of egg-tempera. On some of the dark areas transparent glazes of oil paint were thinly applied.

At the end of six months the mural panels were ready for installation. I had executed them in a loft, a few blocks away from the New School, which Alvin Johnson had procured for me. The panels were removed successfully from the loft, but as they had to be entered horizontally into the third floor window slots of the school and as the movers, not realizing the brittleness of the gesso ground, allowed them to be bent, they got into the Board room in a badly cracked state. At first I thought all my work was lost, but examination showed only a few of the paint surfaces had chipped. After the panels were attached to the wall, I repaired the damages so they were not noticeable except under close scrutiny. However, the cracks were there underneath, and the overall strain to which the panels had been subjected made me uneasy about their future. This was forgotten when, after a few years, no deterioration of the paint surface became evident.

Some twenty-five years later, when on a trip to New York I visited the New School, I found, because of the pressure of students in the constantly growing school, that the Board room had been turned into a classroom and that folding chairs and blackboards were stacked against the surface of the mural. This treatment had evidently been going on for a long time, because very marked lines of abrasion had developed over the mural surface. Abrasions where the chairs had touched and where the tops of the blackboards had scraped were obliterating parts of the basic drawing as well as the surface color. I called this to the attention of Alvin Johnson, who still kept his old interest in the school and maintained offices in the building. He was shocked when he examined the damages, confessing that he had not looked closely at the mural for years. He said that the professors who used the room for their classes were naturally more interested in their subjects than the mural and had probably not noticed the growth of the abrasions either. In any case none had reported anything.

In the end I agreed with Johnson that I would clean the mural, which, in addition to its damages, was streaked with the yearly accumulated dirt of the city, if the New School would put a protective rail about it. This was done, and in the autumn of 1956, I took the old varnish off the surface, repaired the abrasions, and put the work pretty well back into its original shape.

At this time I also made an attempt, with the help of Mario Modestini, of the National Gallery in Washington, to preserve the Orozco murals which were powdering off the walls. The polluted acid-filled air of New York had so acted on Orozco's frescoes that the plaster would not hold the pigment. A wax varnish was applied; but whether it will serve to insulate the murals is still doubtful.

In June of 1968 I again visited the New School to receive an honorary degree. Looking over my mural room, I found that the mural's surface was again frightfully dirty and that most of the restorations I had made in 1956 had chipped off. I was not overly shocked, because a few years back one of my friends, who was expert in the problems of picture preservation, had inspected the work and had warned me that the high temperatures of the mural room would so desiccate the egg-tempera paint films that they would, in time, break up. He said that only the installation of proper air, temperature, and humidity controls in the room would save the mural.

I informed Dr. John Everett, now president of the New School, and its other officials, all of whom were concerned with the preservation of my work, about the need for such museum-like controls. Though they were costly, they were willing to install them.

So in September, 1968, with the help of three very careful and efficient young women artists, which the New School people found for me, I again cleaned the New York muck off the mural surface and repaired the desiccation damages. For reasons completely unknown to me, only certain sections of the mural showed deterioration. Most of the surface, in spite of the assaults of high temperatures and polluted air, was perfectly solid. The behavior of paint films is a mystery that I do not believe even the most expert students of the subject yet understand. I cannot even pretend to do so.

Because of its superior adhesive power, I used an acrylic polymer emulsion paint, instead of egg-tempera, for my second restoration. Fortunately a varnish, removable from such paint, had been made, so the mural can be easily cleaned when, and if, that again becomes necessary—and without affecting my restorations. With the newly controlled conditions in the room I believe the mural will have a long life. But with paint, as with other things, Man proposes, God disposes.

1931 - 1968

With the completion of the New School mural I made the final step into the third phase of my development, which was the application of my methods, by now thoroughly under control, to the scenes, behaviors, and mythologies of American life.

The mural received international attention through reproductions that were widely circulated in European and South American publications. A curiosity abroad about American postwar life had created a readiness to accept the work's environmental explicitness. Reactions against the more and more abstract tendencies of the school of Paris also made its realism acceptable in many quarters. In New York, however, the critical and aesthetic society very largely condemned it. There were two aspects to this dislike of the work—one aesthetic and one political.

The aesthetic objections followed generally the lines indicated before. The attitudes toward art in general, plus the anecdotalism of the mural, were at odds with most of the aesthetic ideas being cultivated in New York's artistic circles. Because the mural depended for its meanings on the simple spectacle of American life and contained no specifically anticapitalist or revolutionary imagery, the radical groups condemned it as "chauvinistic." While during the early and middle twenties I had cultivated a Marxist viewpoint toward capitalist society and had tried to apply it to that of the United States, my growing experience in the field of actual American life and politics had changed my attitudes. The evolution of revolutionary Russia into Stalin's totalitarian and dictatorial society had produced a complete disillusionment in that quarter. What I wanted now was to see clearly the nature of American life as it unrolled before me and to paint it without my vision being distorted by any generalities of social theory. The exposition of this change of mind caused my radical friends to see me with a jaundiced eye. I became for most of them a "reactionary" and a "chauvinist," in addition to again being an "opportunist."

However, there were some people in New York, even in its artistic circles, who took a more favorable view of my effort. One of these was Mrs. Juliana Force, director of the Whitney Museum, who purchased a dozen or more of the drawings made for the New School mural and a year later, in the spring of 1932, commissioned me to do a series of panels for the library of the Whitney.

The theme I chose for Mrs. Force's mural was "The Arts of Life in America," meaning by this the popular arts of the cities and the countryside—the arts practiced by, or directed toward, people in general. I proceeded with the design for this work much as I had with that of the New School, locking the different subject units together on the peripheries of their forms. As I had now become more skillful with this type of composition, I did not need to introduce mouldings or other decorative separations into the design of the mural. I had also become more proficient at composing with clay and knew how to produce perspective illusions with a relatively low relief. I had ceased modelling figures in the complete round, substituting quarter round projections, which not only reduced the physical depth of my sculptures, but permitted a more rapid establishment of rhythmical relations between different parts of my designs. I had learned, in fact, to paint in clay.

Mrs. Force's commission for the Whitney mural stipulated that it be finished in September, which gave me about five months for its planning and execution. The improvement and curtailment of my planning methods was of great help in meeting this commitment. It also vastly expedited another mural, soon to come, where time would be an even greater factor than at the Whitney. I painted this second mural wholly in egg-tempera from drawings and pilot sketches in black and white paint, and I had it ready to "unveil" at the appointed date. Critical reactions were even more adverse than those occasioned by the New School mural. Though I was becoming hardened to this kind of reception, some of it, which came up now, angered me. I was particularly offended when a group of artists—my fellow teachers at the Art Students League—wrote, signed, and published a round-robin letter to one of the New York newspaper critics, applauding him for his condemnation of my work. I have provided accounts of this and related occurrences in other writings, so I need not elaborate on them here.

But when I look back on the atmosphere of animosity toward my painting that took root in these two murals, I am at a loss to explain it. I can't find any sensible reason for it. My ripostes, which grew with the criticisms, did not, of course, help to reduce them; but these defensive replies would not have been delivered at all had I not been goaded into doing so. I think I have correctly assessed the aesthetic and political atmospheres which channelled most of the criticisms levelled at me, but I have never understood their virulence, a virulence which made so many of the artists of New York regularly speak of me as "that son-of-a-bitch Benton." It could not have been jealousy, because all my artist critics were convinced of their own superiority. It could not have been my Americanism alone, because other Americanists, like Burchfield and Hopper, seemed generally acceptable. It could not have been my repudiation of the schools of Paris either, because the Mexican artists, Rivera, Siqueiros, and Orozco, who had also repudiated that school, were everywhere admired. It was not because I questioned the values attributed to "abstract" painting, because a lot of other artists, both here and abroad, were doing likewise. George Grosz, who had put such questions years before I did, had the support of everyone.

Whatever started the chain of criticisms to which I was submitted, they and the replies with which I countered them in the press soon brought me into general public attention. There was at this time an immense regrowth of interest in American history and social behavior, which the depression had accelerated, and this established an intellectual background for the Americanism of my painting. A lot of people rose to my support, and while during the early days of the thirties, artists were everywhere depending on government doles, I was able to sustain myself in a moderate but sufficient fashion by sales of my paintings. So my critics not only built me a reputation, but did me the ultimate favor of providing me with a living.

Because of my improved financial situation, I felt that I was ineligible for participation in one of the most interesting occurrences of our national life—the entrance of the Federal government into the support of art through the Works Progress Administration of the Roosevelt regime. Although a number of artists in New York, who were, like me, above real need, did enter into W.P.A. activities because they saw opportunities for public work—especially mural work—I was already too busy with commissions of this sort from other sources to seek those the government offered. By the time the W.P.A. mural projects were initiated I had all the mural work I could handle.

I had hardly washed my brushes after the completion of the Whitney mural when I was called upon to do another for the State of Indiana's exhibit at the Chicago World's Fair, which was to open on the first of June, 1933. I signed a contract for this early in December of '32, which gave me six months of execution time. The theme of this mural was the "Social History of the State of Indiana." The space to fill was two hundred feet long by twelve feet high, an immense project for so limited a time.

As I had to begin from scratch, knowing nothing of Indiana's history, the first month was given over to research and to travelling over the state to get the "feel" of it. The alignment of my subject matter into progressive sequences and its sculptural and pictorial organization, plus the mass of drawings I had to make, took about a month and a half, so that I was finally left with only a little over three months' time for execution. But working night and day, I got the job done. It is now installed in the auditorium of Indiana University.

Although I was unaware of it, a number of other American artists had, during the twenties, developed a strong Americanist viewpoint and were, like myself, concentrating on the American scene. Among these were John Steuart Curry and Grant Wood, who shared with me a Middle Western background. Probably because of this we began to be associated in the Press as a trio. This began shortly after my Indiana mural was displayed in Chicago, and by the spring of 1934 our association was firmly established and defined by the appellation "Regionalist."

An Americanist environmentalism was already evident in the minds of many American writers who were both reporting about and creating fictional representations of life all over the United States. Coupled with the continuing explorations of such popular historians as Charles Beard and James Truslow Adams, this built up an atmosphere so favorable to the "Regionalist" viewpoint that the Benton, Curry, and Wood trio was catapulted into a premier position in American painting.

This did not, of course, go unchallenged. The same kind of criticism which had been levelled at me when I completed the New School and Whitney murals was now applied to the three of us. We were "reactionary," "chauvinistic," and when it became generally known that we were all Midwesterners, "provincial." However, the public temper of the thirties was with us and nullified the fulminations of our critics. We were successful.

The Indiana mural had publicly reestablished my ties with the Middle West, and a number of my Missouri friends began thinking of ways to set up a Benton mural project for our home state. The first steps for this were taken in the spring of 1934, and the Missouri legislature, under the leadership of State Senator Edward Barbour, passed a bill commissioning a mural for the Capitol in Jefferson City.

I was at this time working on plans for a Treasury Department mural in the new post office in Washington, D. C., and was having difficulties accommodating myself to the views of the Treasury's supervising committee, the aesthetic temper of which was less than sympathetic to my way of doing things. The moment I heard of the passing of the bill for a Benton mural in Missouri, I dropped the post office project flat.

Shortly after this I received an invitation to take over the painting and drawing classes at the Kansas City Art Institute, and with the assurance from the school's directors that my duties there would not be allowed to interfere with work on the Missouri mural project, I moved to Kansas City and established my home there.

The mural space offered in the State Capitol was made up of three walls, one fifty feet long and two of twenty-five feet. The height of the space was sixteen feet. Each wall was cut by a very prominent door, which created designing problems. The walls, where they joined at right angles, brought tricky perspective problems. The only lines or forms which could be made to turn the right angle corners without distortion had to be projected horizontally.

This was the first time in my mural painting experience that I had to contend with an established architectural setting, the shapes of which could not be denied. Whatever I did had to be adjusted to them. It would have been simple enough to handle this situation with flat, decorative forms, but it was difficult with the illusionary three-dimensional projections to which I was now committed.

Like the Indiana mural's theme, this one was also conceived as a social history—"Social History of the State of Missouri"—a depiction of the life, human behaviors, and, of course, the mythology of Missouri. The latter, as was agreed to by the rather liberal-minded Missourians with whom I discussed it, would have to include our great, but somewhat disreputable, heroes—Jesse James, Frankie and Johnny, and Huck Finn. They were the most famous characters spawned in the history of Missouri, and any realistic depiction of the State would have to take them into account. One of the walls was to be given over to the early history of Missouri, but most of the subject matter would deal with a life which was within my experience—memory experience, if not immediate.

After approximately placing the subject sequences in a drawing, I constructed a plastilene model of the whole mural space, setting the doors on the first plane of the design. The actions of the figures also began on this plane, but moved back to planes further in the rear. In order to attach the frames of the doors to the design of the mural and keep them from standing out too much, I continued them illusionarily into the mural space, imitating their color and texture in the final painting. In this way I also produced architectural frames for my representations of Jesse James, Frankie and Johnny, and Huck Finn, since because of their mythical character, I did not want to introduce them into the main, and generally more prosaic, actions of the mural. This preparatory work was carried on in the autumn and winter of 1935-36. By June I had prepared all of the cartoons, figure drawings, and color sketches necessary for final execution. My contractual deadline was January, 1937, but I finished the work in December of '36.

As usual, the "Social History of Missouri" raised a storm of criticism; but this time it did not come from journalistic aesthetes or yowling advocates of revolution, but from good old hidebound, middle-class Missouri conservatives who saw its "common life" representations as an insult to the State. However the mural is still in the State Capitol and has grown so respectable that school children from all over Missouri are now bussed to see it.

The sculptured model of the Missouri mural was the most elaborate and also the largest I had ever made. It was twelve feet long and nearly four feet high, and it took me three months to complete. It differed from other models I had made in that it encompassed the total mural space. The others had been modelled sectionally. Also, for the first time I worked out my general color scheme on the model, painting the different areas with the approximate colors to be used in the mural. The effect of the whole, when completed, was similar to some of the painted reliefs seen in the churches of Italy and Spain. Many people who saw this model deplored the fact that I intended to destroy it after its purpose was served; but as indicated before, I

knew that it was not sculpture and that because of its construction it could not serve as such. I had modelled it on a
basic plane which was tipped back at a forty-five degree
angle. Had that plane been raised to a vertical position, as
would have been necessary for use as architectural decoration, not only would my design have been lost, but all the
forward figures would have appeared to be falling off. I
did not try to set up true sculptural continuities in any of
my models, but only to make a relief map of the projections
and recessions of an illusionary *pictorial* design. I saw the
models only as steps in painting, not as aesthetic products
in themselves.

It is probable that the dioramic sculptures made for
painting purposes by Tintoretto, and others of his time,
were also regarded as only steps in a *compositional* process,
because none of them survive. I have been told that frag-
ments of El Greco's sculptures were preserved at his house
in Toledo, but though I made persistent inquiries about
them on a visit to Toledo in 1954, I did not see any. There
are a number of dioramic sculptures in the cathedrals of
France and Italy (notably effective ones at Chartres) that
suggest paintings, but they were most certainly not made
for producing them. They serve the same function as sculptural pictures or are like miniature stage settings, but are
completely finished products in themselves.

In spite of Vasari's references to the use of clay models
by Renaissance painters and of the present general acceptance of the fact that this practice was widespread, no very
complete investigations, that I know of, have been undertaken to amplify our knowledge of it or of *how* it was carried
on. So many paintings of the late fifteenth and, especially,
sixteenth century have the peculiar concentrated light and
shade of sculptural projections that I am inclined to believe
the practice was general. My own experience has been that
the particular distortions of planes and perspectives necessary in a model that simulates a pictorial space are incom-
patible with true sculpture. This, if generally applicable,
would be enough to account for the fact that no pictorially
directed sculptures by Renaissance artists have lasted. I
usually destroyed those I made as soon as I extracted what
I needed from them. I have found that if they are kept
around, they are disturbing to the completion of a work be-

cause, exactly like the forms of nature, they continually suggest new and different approaches.

I have preserved, in bronze, only one of my painting sculptures, but that is a sectional piece that was modelled upright. An attempt was made in 1961 to cast the sculptured model constructed for the Truman Library mural, but the model was destroyed in the process. So practically nothing remains to show for the many hours and days and weeks I have spent with modelling tools.

Although I painted a number of murals afterwards, I believe the Missouri mural completed the last phase of my development as an artist. While various modifications of my pictorial style were made later—notably the introduction of textural variety in my easel pictures—all the basic structural procedures I would ever use had been arrived at.

In the late thirties and in the forties I became fascinated with Flemish techniques and attempted to introduce them into my painting, but these had little effect on my conceptions. The same was true of the more intensified chiaroscuro of some of the paintings of the forties. It was again true of the added detail of these, which were elaborations rather than modifications of style.

A change of medium from egg-tempera to an acrylic polymer emulsion paint was made in 1960-61 for the Truman Library mural because of the superior toughness of the latter—toughness of the paint film, I mean.

Also, in the Truman mural I introduced for the first time in any of my mural works a single perspective scheme. The Truman mural, occupying one wall, could be fully encompassed from one point of view, so such a scheme was feasible. For all the other murals that I painted, changes of position were necessary for the spectator to take in all of the space. The changes of focus necessarily resulting ruled out single perspectives. While such perspectives facilitate the arrangement and apprehension of forms in depth and help to create spatial illusions, they are not really necessary. Our perceptions of depth come more from the superpositioning of objects—from our *recognition* that one is behind or forward of another—than from following their perspective lines. We most certainly do not *perceive* our visual worlds through the *laws* of perspective. Therefore, I never felt any need to adhere to them while constructing my other mural compositions. The prime objective was to create a "flow" of form from one area of the mural to another so that the "unity of the whole" could be *empathically* apprehended. I set up a single-perspective scheme in the Truman mural largely because the architectural situation created problems that I thought it might help solve.

The reader of this account will have noticed that the word "problem" has been frequently used. It could well appear that my interest in art has been largely absorbed by problems. From the technical point of view taken in most of this writing, this aspect of my development does stand out quite prominently. I don't see how it could be otherwise, for technical problems did exist and did need solutions. I faced them over and over from the very beginning, as I tried to adjust the various methods I adopted to the various meanings I wanted to express. In my mural art, which I started in 1919 and which was the core of my painting for most of the forty years following, organizational problems were constant factors. The appearance of a mural painting when you are working close to it on a scaffold is quite different from its appearance when you get down on the floor and take the spectator's point of view. You can't change your mind up on a scaffold without the risk of everything going awry. You must solve your problems before you get up there.

The "flow" of form, mentioned above, which creates the unity of a mural, does not come by itself. Once started, however, it does grow, sometimes almost of its own accord, but it is just as likely to grow in the wrong direction as not and leave you with an unmanageable situation. So, again, the growth of a mural design must be controlled from the start. Every inch of it must be planned beforehand, its effects pre-calculated far more than those of an easel picture.

But even had I remained solely an easel painter, I would have had problems. The art of our century is itself a problem. It has, by and large, tended to become a progression of abstractions, one growing out of the other in much the same way that machines grow out of each other, but without the prolonged usage value of these. Of course something like this has been true throughout all the history of art—forms do grow out of forms, but never before has this growth been so turned in on itself as to completely dehumanize the results. This curious development began with Cézanne's efforts to re-create the articulated images of Classical and Renaissance art which impressionistic naturalism had well nigh obliterated. In the place of a fragmented pictorial world, Cézanne sought a unified one. His procedures led to a new concern with the abstract properties of art, the inherent dynamics of lines, shapes, and colors in conjunction. Whereas Cézanne used these abstract properties in the interest of a better representation of nature—for a human purpose, that is—those who followed him used them simply for themselves. At least that has been so largely the case since about 1910 that it must be judged the predominant trend of our century.

It is true that American art especially in Mexico and the United States was almost completely taken over during the twenties and thirties by representational subject painting. For at least fifteen years of that time those abstractionists who regard this rehumanization as derogatory to art's "independent" status held a secondary position. Nevertheless the trend toward abstraction, though submerged, continued and again became dominant after the Second World War. A similar situation obtained in Germany. The famous draughtsman George Grosz grew out of a German regionalist movement somewhat akin to American Regionalism though it was not sustained for so long a period. It was also submerged in "abstractionist" trends.

In late years I have often been asked how long artists would continue to occupy themselves with "abstract" experiments. As the possibilities for combinations of lines, colors, and shapes are almost infinite, this could, theoretically speaking, go on forever. I think this question will, however, be answered by society. When the powers of society again find a function for the artist and put him again to representing society's meanings, the directions of art will change. The communicative challenge will again be uppermost. The "art for art's sake" movements, of which "abstractionism" is only one, are to a large extent like defenses built up to compensate for society's negligence of, and indifference to, the artist. By stating the independence of art from communicative demands, the artist states his own independence of the need of them. If society, seeing him as a useless relic of the past, thumbs its nose at him, he thumbs his own back.

Though I have very positively rejected this abstractionist trend and have refused to abandon the historic representational purposes of art in my own work, I am quite willing to admit that some interesting and at least momentarily attractive objects have come out of it.

If these objects had been regarded for what they are—simply as more or less decorative combinations of line, color, and shape—most of my public difficulties with our "abstractionists" would never have developed.

I have myself spent a great deal of time working with the basic properties of art, combining purely geometric forms. In my case, however, the resulting combinations were not themselves what we call ends. The ends I had in view, once I arrived at some control of my methods, were always to create effective vehicles for representing and communicating meanings.

I have never opposed or criticized anybody's concern with abstract designing per se. On the contrary, because of the essentially constructive nature of the art object, I have always asserted the necessity of some geometric, or abstract, designing. I have only said that without some meaningful purpose such designing must end simply as a decorative art. And I still think that is so. There is nothing wrong, of course, with a decorative art. Some of the most beautiful objects man has created have been made for purely decorative purposes. But I do think it is wrong to say that this is the only kind of art appropriate for our time, as do so many of its protagonists.

Contrary to general belief, the "Regionalist" movement did not in any way oppose abstract form. It simply wished to put meanings, recognizable American meanings, into some of it. In my own case I had, in addition to the conviction that American meanings were necessary for an American art, a further conviction that purely abstract designing could not produce memorable forms. Over the years my observations of paintings and sculptures had impressed on my mind a great number of precise memory images. Simply by closing my eyes I could recall the formal particularities of dozens of pictorial and sculptural representations.

This is not true of our modern abstract forms. Though I have seen hundreds of them and have looked with interest, and even pleasure, on many, the only one which has had enough impact to be precisely remembered is Marcel Duchamp's "Nude Descending the Staircase." This is the only one—the rest are all blurs and are recalled, if at all, not as forms but because of the theories they represented.

For the semi-abstract forms which retain a touch of humanistic suggestiveness, such as Pablo Picasso's "Lady at Her Toilet" in New York's Museum of Modern Art and some of Giorgio de Chirico's paintings, the case is a little better. But even with these my memory recalls are vague when compared with those occasioned by Botticelli's "Venus," Grant Wood's "American Gothic," John Curry's "Line Storm," Roger Van der Weyden's "Deposition" in Madrid's Prado, or El Greco's "Nativity" in New York's Metropolitan Museum, to name but a few remembered works.

If this is the case for a trained professional eye, how much more so must it be for the untrained public eye. As it is through, and by, the memorable impacts its forms occasion that art functions socially, makes its meanings publicly effective, it appears that the purely abstract arts of our time must be relegated to the status of passing novelties. Without sustained effectiveness on the mind, they cannot have a sustained life—even for artists. This was the conclusion that cemented my own final attachment to representational forms. Born in the "show me" State of Missouri and having a fair amount of respect for my family traditions there, I wanted my performances to have some public effect —be more than mere flickers in a social vacuum.

SELECTED PAINTINGS | by Thomas Hart Benton

Chestnut Tree—"Contre Soleil"
1910   Collection of the Artist

Self Portrait
1909   Collection of the Artist

81

Portrait of the Artist's Sister
1913   Collection of the New Britain Museum of
American Art, New Britain, Connecticut

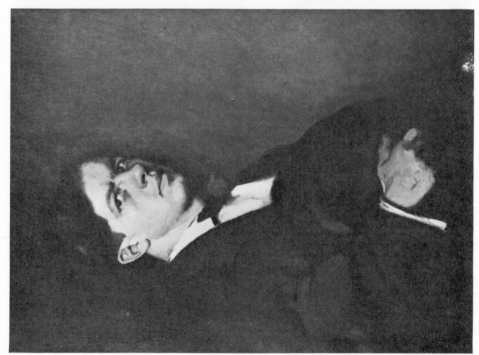

Self Portrait
1912   Collection of the Artist

Palisades, Hudson River
1917   Collection of Beatrice Ornstein, New York City

Constructivist Still Life
1917-18   Collection of the Columbus Gallery of Fine Arts, Columbus, Ohio

Garden Scene (Figure Composition)
1918-19   Collection of Mrs. Sarah Hunt Kelly, New York City

Prayer (Historical Series)
1920-21   Collection of the Artist

The Lord Is My Shepherd
1920-21   Collection of the Whitney Museum of American Art, New York

The Planters (Historical Series)
1921-22   Collection of the Artist

The City (New York Scene)
1923   Collection of the Artist

Self Portrait
1925   Collection of the Artist

Bootleggers
1926-27   Collection of the Artist

Rita and T. P.
1928   Collection of Thomas Piacenza Benton

Cotton Loading (Red River Landing, La.)
1928   Collection of the Artist

Boomtown

1928   Collection of the Memorial Art Gallery of the University of
Rochester, the Marion Stratton Gould Fund

Louisiana Rice Fields

1928   Collection of the Brooklyn Museum, Brooklyn, New York

Homestead

1928   Collection of the Museum of Modern Art, Gift of Marshall Field

Cotton Pickers, Georgia
1928-29   Collection of the Metropolitan Museum of Art,
George A. Hearn Fund, 1933

Arts of Life Mural, City Activities with Dancehall
1930   The New School for Social Research, New York City

Arts of Life Mural, City Activities with Subway
1930   The New School for Social Research, New York City

Arts of the City Mural
1932   Collection of the New Britain Museum of American Art,
New Britain, Connecticut

Arts of the West Mural
Collection of the New Britain Museum of American Art,
New Britain, Connecticut

1932

Chicago World Fair—1933
1933   Collection of Thomas Piacenza Benton

Indiana Mural, Section
1933   Auditorium, Indiana University

Jealous Lover of Lone Green Valley
1934   Collection of the University of Kansas Art Museum

Portrait of Carl Ruggles
*1934   Collection of the William Rockhill Nelson Gallery,
Kansas City, Missouri*

Lord, Heal the Child
1934   Collection of George Perutz, Dallas, Texas

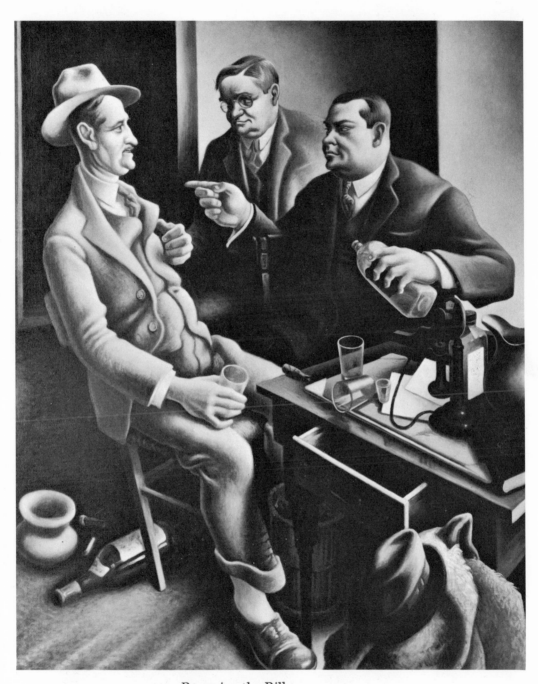

Preparing the Bill

1934   Collection of American Painting, Randolph-Macon Woman's College,
Lynchburg, Virginia

Missouri Mural, Section
1936 Capitol, Jefferson City, Missouri

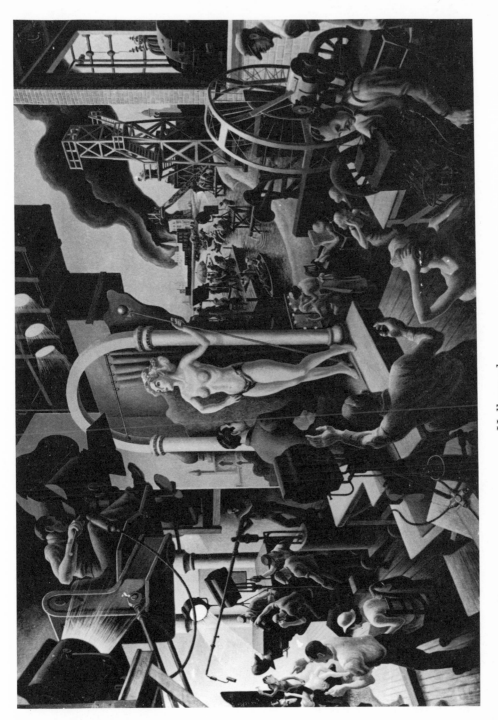

Hollywood

1937   Collection of the Artist

Roasting Ears

1938-39   Collection of the Metropolitan Museum of Art, Arthur H. Hearn Fund, 1939

Cradling Wheat

1938   Collection of the City Art Museum of Saint Louis

Missouri Spring (Flood of 1937)
1938-early 1940's   Collection of Harpo Marx

T. P. and Jake

1938   Collection of Thomas Piacenza Benton

Threshing Wheat

1938-39   Courtesy, Sheldon Swope Art Gallery, Terre Haute, Indiana

Susannah and the Elders
1938   Collection of the California Palace of the Legion of Honor,
San Francisco, California

Persephone
1939   Collection of Rita P. Benton

Cotton Weighing

1939   Collection of the Honorable and Mrs. True Davis,
St. Joseph, Missouri

Negro Soldier

1941   State Historical Society of Missouri, Columbia, Missouri

Jessie and Jake

1942   Collection of Jessie Benton

Gateside Conversation

Early 1940's   Collection of John Paxton, Fort Worth, Texas

July Hay

1942-43   Collection of the Metropolitan Museum of Art,
George A. Hearn Fund, 1943

The Music Lesson

1943   Collection of Mrs. Mary Koch, Wichita Art Museum, Wichita, Kansas

Jazz Boy
Mid-1940's   Collection of the Museum of Art and Archaeology, University of
Missouri, Columbia, Missouri

Fire in the Barnyard
Mid-1940's   Collection of Hubert Strauss, Houston, Texas

Still Life with Rose
Mid-1940's   Collection of Rita P. Benton

Wreck of Ole '97

Mid-1940's   Collection of Mr. and Mrs. Louis D. Cohen, Great Neck, New York

Rice Threshing, La.
Mid-1940's   Collection of the Artist

Achelous and Hercules Mural, Section
1946   Harzfeld's, Kansas City, Missouri

Photographing the Bull
1946 Collection of Ralph Ritter, Kansas City, Missouri

Poker Night

1948   The Joan and Lester Avnet Collection, New York

Lincoln University Mural
1954-55   Lincoln University, Jefferson City, Missouri

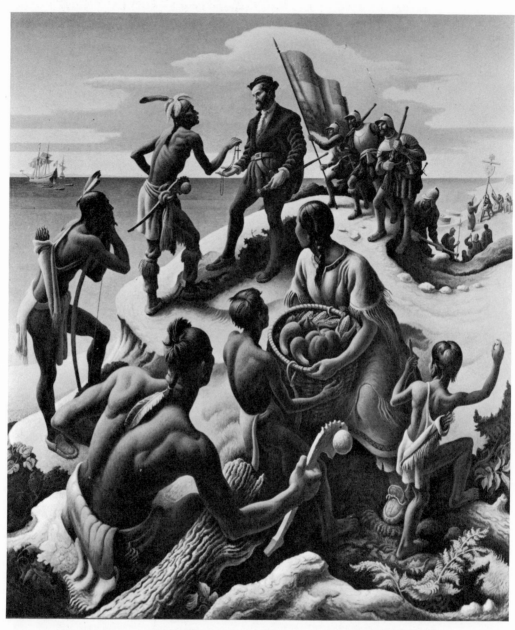

Jacques Cartier on the St. Lawrence
1956   Power Authority of the State of New York

The Bicyclers

Mid-1950's *Collection of Jessie Benton*

Old Kansas City Mural

1956 The River Club, Kansas City, Missouri

The Sheepherder

1955-60   Collection of Mr. and Mrs. Fred W. McCraw, Kansas City, Missouri

Jessie with Guitar
1957   Collection of Jessie Benton

Father Hennepin at Niagara

1961   Power Authority of the State of New York

135

Truman Library Mural, Section
1961   The Harry S. Truman Library, Independence, Missouri

Truman Library Mural

1961   The Harry S. Truman Library, Independence, Missouri

The Young Fisherman
Early 1960's   Collection of Thomas Piacenza Benton

The Twist Dancers
1964   Collection of the Artist

139

Jessie and Anthony
1965 Collection of Jessie Benton

Trial by Jury
1965-66   Collection of Rita P. Benton

141

Ten Pound Hammers
1965-66   Collection of the Artist

Lewis and Clark at Eagle Creek
1966-67   Collection of the Artist

143

Discussion

1967   Collection of John W. Callison, Kansas City, Missouri

AMERICAN REGIONALISM

A Personal History of the Movement

AMERICAN REGIONALISM

A Personal History of the Movement

Quite a number of artists in the late twenties were engaged in looking at the American scene. Burchfield, Hopper, Marsh, and still others less publicly known had turned away from European influences and were seeking their artistic salvation in home experience. The way of George Bellows, the early John Sloan, and Thomas Eakins was being revived after the novelties of the famous Armory Show of 1913 had worn off. An Americanist movement, though it was not clearly defined, was in the air.

In the early thirties this movement was given public dramatization, spotlighted, and held up to national attention in the persons of Grant Wood, John Steuart Curry, and myself. How or why this first occurred is hard to say. In the beginning it appears to have been just a turn of chance, though later, as I will show, some good reasons for it developed. Perhaps we caught the public fancy because we were associated with the Middle West where, it was generally supposed, art was something out of place and, in spite of George Caleb Bingham and the old cultivations of plantation life, without any precedent. However it occurred, and it was first through the couplings of Eastern rather than Western writers, we came, as a Midwestern trio, to spearhead what was called American Regionalism. The Middle West, our home country, became the home of American Regionalism. And the Middle Western subject matter we so often used became recognized as the special identifying property of this Regionalism.

The name Regionalism was taken, I believe, from a group of southern writers, poets, and essayists, who in the late twenties called themselves "agrarians." These, turning from the over-mechanized, over-commercialized, over-cultivated life of our metropolitan centers, were seeking *the sense* of American life in its sectional or regional cultures. It was applied to Wood, Curry, and me with some degree of fitness but mainly, I suspect, because the fashions of the time called for classifications. In painting circles of New York you were, or had been after the Armory Show cataloguing of 1913 occurred, Impressionist, Neo-Impressionist, Fauvist, Cubist, Constructionist, Vorticist, Synchromist, or you were allied in some way to one of these, mostly French inspired, groups. A name had to be found for us.

But this Regionalism was not a clear term. Neither Wood, Curry, nor I ever held ourselves, either in space or time, to any American region.

It is true that we painted many pictures of the rural life of the Midwest but the Midwest is not a single region but many regions—each with its own peculiar cultural character. The difference between the adjoining states of Missouri and Kansas is immense. Kansas towns are western, Missouri towns largely southern. In Missouri itself the cotton cultures of the southeast, the Ozark woods and hill cultures of the middle south, the race horse and mule raising cultures of the center, the stock raising and diversified farming cultures of the north and west are all different. The name Regionalism suggested too narrow a range of inspiration to be quite applicable. We went from place to place, from scene to scene, from region to region, from one time period to another.

This was particularly true of my case. I was after a picture of America in its entirety. The regionalism of the southern agrarians was anti-industrial and as I have said anti-metropolitan. A large part of my own work had been concerned with industrial and metropolitan factors. I ranged north and south and from New York to Hollywood and back and forth in legend and history.

Shortly after writing the first draft of this paper, I attended a three day symposium on the historical work of Frederick J. Turner, held at the University of Kansas City. Stretched along the back wall of the theatre in which the discussions occurred were the first ten original panels of the "History of the United States" which I commenced in 1919 and worked on through the twenties and which I had loaned to the University. These and the subsequent histories I painted of the States of Indiana and Missouri, in which representations of frontier conditions were predominant and proclamatory of a belief in their high significance, had long since publicly connected me with Turner's conceptions. In the various historical societies of the Mississippi valley, whose meetings I had attended, either as talker or listener, I was generally regarded as a sort of Turner in paint. When I spoke it was in language reflective of Turnerite conceptions. At the University of Kansas City symposium I, therefore, expressed my indebtedness to Turner. And debt I had.

However, the concept of our society as an evolution from primitivism to technology through a succession of peoples' frontiers which sparked my first attempts at painting American history pre-dated my knowledge of Turner. At least I think it did. My original purpose was to present a peoples' history in contrast to the conventional histories which generally spotlighted great men, political and military events, and successions of ideas. I wanted to show that the peoples' behaviors, their *action* on the opening land, was the primary reality of American life. Of course this was a form of Turnerism, but it was first suggested to me by Marxist-Socialist theory which, as I show later, was very much in my mind when I turned from a French-inspired studio art to one of the American environment. This socialist theory treated "operations" and "processes" as more fundamental than "ideas." It also maintained the theoretical supremacy of the "people." I had in mind, following this theory, to show that America had been made by the "operations of people" who as civilization and technology advanced became increasingly separated from the benefits thereof. I would go in my history from the frontiers, where the people controlled operations, to the labor lines of the machine age, where they decidedly did not.

It is possible that Turner's history had affected me indirectly when I started my own history, but I do not remember reading his famous essay until after I had come well along with my work, that is, at about 1927 or 1928. After this, and especially in the commissioned histories of Indiana and Missouri, I was without question under Turner's influence. However, the "visual facts" which I experienced directly in these two states and the folk myths which went with them would have been enough, I believe, to make me paint as I did. Whatever one may think of the rough "unidealistic" frontierisms of which these murals are so full, however one may evaluate them, I am convinced that no realistic histories, such as mine tried to be, could have avoided stressing their importance. They were too obvious in the actual cultures represented. The pattern of frontier behaviors and the folk images growing therefrom which I pictured as the fundamental realities of Missouri life led me to the remark which so shocked Missouri respectables in 1937. "I had not," I said, "included the famous Missouri-born General Pershing in my history because he was not important there, not even as important as an ordinary Missouri mule."

Some kind of a general environmentalism might have better covered the cases of Wood, Curry, and me. But that would not have done either. To the French philosopher Taine, all art was environmentalist, conditioned, that is, in form and spirit by the particulars of the places and cultures in which it was made. If this was true, and I most certainly believe it was and must always be where art has depth, then the term was too general. Wood, Curry, and I thought of ourselves simply as American or Americanist painters, sectional at one moment, national and historical at others. If we dealt largely with "agrarian" subjects, it was because these were significant parts of our total American experience. Surely man and the earth were not so new to art that our returns thereto needed a special name.

However, the milk was spilt. Regionalists we became and the victims thereby of a lot of odd and inaccurate definitions which the word suggested. "Regional" and "provincial" were made synonymous for our cases. Old European comparisons of the backward "provincial" and the progressive "metropolitan" were hauled out of their dusty sacks to ridicule us. Critics and painters who were caught in the toils of modern Parisian aestheticism and other intellectual imports, and who were apparently totally ignorant of the historic character of American development, where peripheral forces have been so enormously significant for our culture, saw us as narrow, backward, European-like peasants. This confusion of the roles of the metropolitan centers of

Europe, where social and institutional changes went out-
wards to the provinces, with that of like centers in America,
where these changes just as often came backwards from
forces operating on the frontier, was in spite of its absurdity
enough to tag our American regionalism as a *provincial*
movement. In everyday American that meant a "hick"
movement. As such, however, criticism boomeranged, and
what was meant to slaughter us helped draw to us a national attention and sympathy. We came in the popular
mind to represent a home-grown, grass-roots artistry which
damned "furrin" influence and which knew nothing about
and cared nothing for the traditions of art as cultivated city
snobs, dudes, and assthetes knew them. A play was written
and a stage erected for us. Grant Wood became the typical
Iowa small towner, John Curry the typical Kansas farmer,
and I just an Ozark hillbilly. We accepted our roles.

Actually the three of us were pretty well educated,
pretty widely read, had had European training, knew what
was occurring in modern French art circles, and were tied
in one way or another to the main traditions of Western
painting. What distinguished us from so many other American painters of our time was not a difference in training or
aesthetic background but a desire to redirect what we had
found in the art of Europe toward an art specifically representative of America. This involved first a dissolution of the
contemporary European ban on the stressing of subject
matter. After we had made the dissolution, we were forced
to by-pass contemporary European, or rather Parisian, painting fashions and seek our technical resources further back
in history where, as we knew, subject matter had been an
important aesthetic factor. Thirdly, we had to find, *and*
think in, aesthetic terms applicable to the representation of
a culture in a thousand ways different from that of Europe.

None of this had we planned, or agreed upon, as a
group. In other places I have told of some of my own
separate searchings and findings.* Wood and Curry also
made their discoveries and came to their conclusions separately. I met John Curry in 1929 or 1930. He, it is true,
had read my article "Form and the Subject" published in
The Arts magazine in 1924, but, as his work shows, had already come to similar opinions. I met Grant Wood in

* *An Artist in America.*

1934. He had read none of my writings and of my work had seen only the Indiana mural at the Chicago World's Fair in 1933. Although our names were coupled as Midwestern painters some time before my return to Missouri in 1935, it was only after that time that we began seeing one another and cementing by personal contact our publicly advertised bonds. With Curry established for his long stay as artist in residence at the University of Wisconsin, with Wood at the University of Iowa, and with myself established in Kansas City, we found week-end visits fairly easy to make. Our closer acquaintance revealed that we were not so close to one another as the attachment of our names indicated. We were decidedly different both in temperament and experience and, because of that, in our conceptions of art. We were particularly different in our definitions of the very American realism which we all publicly advocated.

Realism for me, once beyond the matter of subject, was largely technical, having to do with the spatial position of objects and their projection in a three-dimensional scheme. Theoretically, at least, this could have been advanced with geometrical solids, but at the cost of abandoning the American meanings on which I depended, not only for publicly apprehensible content, but for aesthetic stimulation. This realism tried to symbolize the turmoil of America by setting up a turmoil of rhythmic sequences and it got along, at least up to 1938, without subtleties of texture, natural color, or atmospheric light, in fact without any subtleties.

Realism for Wood, in the way of the Flemish and Dutch genre painters to whom he was devoted, entailed a close study of natural texture and local color coupled with a detailed rendering of all the specially characteristic parts of objects represented. He could, for instance, simplify a garment but would not be satisfied unless buttons, buckles, pockets, etc., were authentic in detail. This went along with a schematic design drawn partly from the Gothic stained glass window, the techniques of which he had studied thoroughly for his own work in the glass field, and partly from old English and American china painting. To the apparent contradictions between his decorative and two-dimensional compositional techniques and his visual, sometimes photographic objectivity, Wood could, and did, point to the solutions of similar contradictions so splendidly made in the period of transition between Gothic and Renaissance styles in Northern Europe. Against the tumult of America to which my concepts of realism were aimed, Wood set a concept expressive of the contained quiet, sly humor, and political conservatism of the well-groomed, long-settled and ordered Iowa town. Whatever he painted reflected this quiet. There was none of the frontier adventurer in Wood.

The realism of John Curry was technically simpler than either mine or Wood's but it was psychologically more complex. Curry had come into painting after a trial at American style illustration which meant, of course, in the early part of the century the accurate and rather photographic visualization of a text. Aesthetic or formal considerations were secondary to that and particularly so in the magazine field which Curry tried to enter. The text was first and must be faithfully represented. When Curry turned from trying to represent fictional *texts*, at which he was but moderately successful, to representing directly experienced *subjects* in the larger field of painting, he carried with him the feeling that it was necessary to be faithful first and foremost. Faithful to "what was there" took the place of to "what was described," but the attitude was the same. Perhaps it was an inherent sense of this faithfulness, pre-dating his illustrative experience and set deep in his basic character, which really checked Curry as an illustrator and sent him into painting. It was not in his serious temperament to go rapidly and superficially from one thing to another as the illustrative trade necessarily demanded. No doubt he tended to be too profoundly faithful for the work. In any case Curry's realism as it first developed after his abandonment of illustrations was driven by an inner conviction that he must be absolutely true to his subject and to the visual conditions in which that subject manifested itself. The meaning of the subject was found by hunting out and representing faithfully its main visual characteristics. This seems a simple, direct, and logical realism. However, it was untenable in technical practice, and because he held to it as a sort of doctrine, it set up a series of lifelong conflicts in John Curry's soul.

To anyone familiar with art and with the primary necessity it imposes that some kind of logical integration of parts be set up, where formal relations have to be substituted for "natural" ones, the difficulties of Curry's doctrinal position should be obvious. These difficulties were compounded when he went into historical subject matter with his mural work. The old struggle between *experience* and *form*, *meaning* and *form*, was more acute in John Curry's mind than in that of any artist I have ever known. He had in himself a lot of the tortured earnestness of the Scotch Covenanters and was, in fact, descended from these. His immediate family was intensely religious. He was not inclined, as were Wood and I, to indulge his art very much in satire or humor. Technically his realism was closely allied to the mid-nineteenth century visual realism of Courbet, Winslow Homer, Thomas Eakins, and the broader manifestations of Impressionism.

At least this was so at first. Later and during the time in which I knew him, when he was trying to extend his technical resources, he was an avid student of High Renaissance painting, particularly that of Rubens—whose work had always fascinated him—and the Venetians. He had, however, a dislike of the rhythmical sequences of Baroque art, to which I was so attracted, regarding them, Calvinist like, as "artificial" and "untrue." Curry honestly tried to believe, even after he began using obvious compositional artifices, that he "painted what he saw" or historically "what could have been seen." Of the three of us, he certainly came nearest to that "ideal," and maybe, therefore, the nearest to a picture of our actual America. I don't know. Beliefs that are illusory often result in things which are truest.

Now in the course of our association and for all our differences of view and temperament, Wood, Curry, and I began influencing one another. We were not aware of this, but little by little there came about some reciprocal tradings. It was after studying Wood's pictures that I became interested in textural detail. Studying Curry, I tried to get closer to actual visual appearances and to everyday happenings. Both Wood and Curry began taking over from my work our increased concern with three-dimensional geometric structure. Some of Wood's late lithographs were almost sculptural.

Curry was the least affected in this trading, but it is

notable that his Wisconsin still lifes became more and more decorative, silhouetted like Wood's, and that he began to design his large subject pictures with more and more attention to Baroque-like rhythmical sequences. The difference between his "Kansas Baptism" painted in 1928 and his later mural paintings indicates his technical shift. However, these tradings were minor and affected no substantial modifications in our styles. Had we met earlier in life we might have made a true school. As it was, we remained individually and technically different.

Nevertheless we were attached to one another by ideas which overrode our technical and definitional differences. These, which not only bound us together but separated us from contemporary art trends in France and from those in America which were like them, were first our attitudes toward the place of subject matter in the formative process and secondly our views as to the purpose of art in society. The first of these I have mentioned, but I must here re-emphasize it. We all held that *what* was painted should determine, as far as possible, the *how* of its painting and the ultimate form that ensued. In this view ways and means were secondary to content in the building of significant forms. We knew that this sounded like Victorianism. But we were willing to face that issue. Against the better part of the theorists of our time we redefined the word *significant* and returned it from the technical field, where it had come to indicate a functional relationship between the parts of a design, back into a public field where it meant meaning for the spectator. Otherwise put, we were bent on returning painting to its historic representational purpose and, further, in the interests of an American art, to making it represent matter drawn from American life and meaningful to those living that life.

If subject matter determined *form* and the subject matter was distinctively American, then we believed an American form, no matter what the source of technical means, would eventually ensue. If this form had public significance, and we felt from our own experiences that it must, then a public demand for it would grow. Art would thus come to function in American life and the American artist would find himself no more a mere exhibitor before society, after the way of French salonism with its commercial adjunct, the precious picture gallery, but a creator within society, paid like a good workman for purposeful work.

We could point to several artistic manifestations in our past culture which seemed corroborative of our views. There was the popular portraiture from Colonial times up to about 1830 which often possessed novel and American-looking departures from European portrait conventions. There was the art of George Caleb Bingham, also immensely popular, which had asserted an American way of composing the American scene and of handling light effects in the days just before and after the Civil War. Most notable were the popular Currier and Ives prints where traditional techniques, both material and organizational and all of European origin, had developed through environmental subject matter into an art which was unmistakably American and which could not have been made save in America. We could see that these popular art forms had, for all their limitations, turned out to be the most distinctive forms of their day as well as the most reflective of America. Where the "high" art of the Hudson River school, which prevailed at the same time, ran more frequently than not into a rank imitation of European models, the "low" popular print art kept an indigenous character and gave promise of original form.

Let your American environment, we concluded, be your source of inspiration, American public meaning your purpose, and an art will come which will represent America before the world and be acclaimed and supported by Americans as a proof at last that they are culturally on their own.

This dream, and dream it has turned out to be, fitted however, with certain other dreams growing in American society during the period when Wood, Curry, and I, unknown to each other, were forming ourselves. It seems to me now, looking back, that we were perhaps only the aesthetic spearheads of something much wider and deeper than art which rose gropingly in American society during the twenties and which in the thirties took the positive form of a new Americanist idealism. Our success, I believe, was closely attached to this. We were, if not always in a completely harmonious way, identified with widespread

American thoughts and feelings. Our aesthetic American-ism expressed a social Americanism.

The slogan "America First," because of its attachment to some of the worst and most irresponsible demagoguery our country has ever known, possesses an ugly sound today. We must, however, not let that blind us to the fact that it had always been a fundamental concept of American nationalism as that was politically expressed, and that further it was the very reason for the existence of that nationalism. The separation from England resulted from an economic "America Firstism" and not from any idealistic theory of government. The latter came after, when the lines of economic conflict had passed the breaking point. Whatever American idealism came to say, and it said a lot, the practical American politician never let go the sense that America and American interests came first. And in that, save during the break of the Civil War, he always had behind him the whole effective population of the country. "America First" was and is deep-rooted in the popular American mind. Does this exemplify some particularly American chauvinism? Hardly. What about the history of England First, or of France First, or of Germany First, or today of the world-disturbing Russia First? Let's not let our notions of what an internationalist "ought to be" confuse us here. Also let us not forget that in their domestic fronts these "firsts" were not and are not all evil. This includes even Russia—and China.

"America First" along with other "firsts" has had its idealistic aspects. As it concerns this writing, it rose to a sudden and renewed strength immediately after the First World War when the failure of Woodrow Wilson's world idealism before the brute chauvinisms of Clemenceau and the English vengeance complexes of Lloyd George became apparent. The dissolution of the Wilsonian democratic world dream before the loot hungers of Europe forced America promptly back on herself. There was a wholesale return to her own loot problems. Who was to have and what? Not in the world, but in America.

The initial moves here were atrocious. The turn from world idealism crushed all idealism. While Wilson, defeated, lay dying, every democratic and humane idea he stood for, not only on the international but on the domestic front, seemed to die too. Labor, under the illusion that its Wilsonian gains meant something practical, had its head beaten to a pulp. Business pretenses that labor strikes for better wage conditions represented the new bolshevism of Russia and the destruction of all property rights were taken up by the press and turned into a national dogma. Ordinary "run of the mine" gradualists, socialists, political innocents —the most of them—were knocked in the head right and left. Wilson's own Attorney-General Palmer, with no sanction whatever from his disabled leader, gave himself a field day of repressive violence which virtually destroyed all that his party had lately initiated. Something approaching revolutionary conditions arose in America because labor and a number of progressive politicians and labor leaders who remembered the American dream and Wilson's promises about it fought back, and with a good deal of intellectual support. But in very ill-advised and unthought out moves coal miners and railroad workers came out for nationalization of their industries and put heavy weapons in the hands of those who believed that "America First" meant "Business and Propertied Privilege First."

In the northwestern part of the country and in areas still dominated by the social concepts of frontierism, I.W.W. advocates of "One Big Union lined up against Capital" put further weapons in the hands of the "Business and Property First" crowd. Left-wing Socialist plans for mass action and the general strike added to these. Hoodlum-conducted violences during the famous strike of the unionized Boston police instigated a hatred of all unionism among the majority of propertied people. To this divisive turmoil were added race riots and race and religious hatreds. The Ku Klux Klan with its anti-Negro, anti-Jew, and anti-Catholic platform stalked, white-robed and sinister, over the land. It had its own form of "America First."

For nearly two years violence and counterviolence ruled over the postwar return of America to itself. Then, somehow, all quieted down. Prices were high. Goods in a war-depleted country were desperately needed. Business, however reactionary politically, had radical techniques to produce them. The war had shown how to organize mass production. "Business First" won out. The fear of revolution died. After all, as later figures showed, less than three-tenths of one per cent of the population entertained social ideas of an extreme nature.

Under "Business First" auspices the "normalcy" of President Harding took the country in hand. "Normalcy" meant not America first in any liberalist sense, or even productive business first, but very largely "Profits, and the Public Be Damned, First," even the stock holding public. However, in spite of scandal mounted on scandal—Teapot Dome, the War Veterans Bureau, the Ohio gang, the finances of the Republican party, which later stained even the high respectability of the "greatest secretary of the treasury since Hamilton"—prosperity returned to America and the "let 'er roll" psychology of a world in boom became nationally prevalent. Hurrah for the American way! What if it did involve a little robbery, graft, and rascality, it was successful. So successful indeed that under the "Business First" regime of Coolidge, which followed Harding's, even Europe took notice and bowed to the superiority of the new American social techniques. Even a French historian, André Siegfried, could in *America Comes of Age* write of them with a touch of something like envy.

By no means isolationist, "Business First" reached out over the world. American money was invested in every foreign project that even slightly suggested the possibility of profit. American financiers, engineers, and industrialists were called on everywhere for their new "know-how." This international confidence in the "American way" bolstered its success at home. New industries boomed, the automobile took the country, and roads, bridges, dams, and gigantic office buildings loomed up almost overnight. The release of energy was terrific and, even to those who like myself did not share much in its benefits, inspiring. What person, sensitive to human drama, could have helped being stirred by this "devil take the hindmost" race, this display of power, immense greed, and superhuman confidence?

But the play, as we all know, came to its climax. It ended in the tragedy of 1929, and one form of Americanism retired for a while from the stage. Not all forms however. Even during the days of boom, concepts other than those of Business as to what constituted the American way persisted. What had been good for business and also for the better part of industrial labor, which lost its radicalism under the flow of boom dollars, had not been good for farmers and for thousands of small-town middlemen and their workers who depended on the prosperity of farmers. For these people the "Business First" way didn't spell out a satisfactory American Way. Down South, in the Middle West and in the Northwest, discontent prevailed. And there were spokesmen for this discontent. And men ready to capitalize on it. The old American question, always fearfully radical to the Kings of business, "Where do we, the people, of America come in?" found men ready to answer it as the boom reached its close and labor found itself in the same plight with the farmers. They had been around all the time, these men, not taking part, but hanging in the wings of the great play. And there were many of them. Notably all the ambitious members of the Democratic party who had been pretty much left out in the cold under Harding, Coolidge, and Hoover. They had a lot to say. In addition to these was a body of able and influential writers, scholars, and intellectuals, who had never from its beginning felt happy about a businessman's culture. And there were a lot of old-fashioned religious people who didn't like to see Jesus Christ elected head of the advertising clan and made to sponsor cigarettes, lipsticks, transparent stockings, and other paraphernalia of the devil. And there was the "lost generation," the young, who had drunk, smoked, and petted themselves to satiation during the boom hoopla and were looking at last for a decent place to nurse their shredded souls and for some kind of an ideal to cling to.

In the very midst, nay at the very beginning, of the great show there were many Americans who looked skeptically about them. The success of Sinclair Lewis' 1920 novel *Main Street* is ample proof of this. Lewis, Dreiser, Anderson, and others who turned their spotlights on the realities of the cultural scene that "Business First" created, lacked no readers. Beneath the wild dance of the time there was always a ferment of thought and a lot of sharp observation to cut through the trappings of boom time success into the real things below. Most of those we regard today as our great modern American writers began their careers then.

Now the notable thing about these literary people and the scholars, too, who looked skeptically with them at what was going on in America is that they kept their eyes on the country, no matter how little they liked it. A great crowd of lesser scribes, particularly those afflicted with "high-brow-ism," did in the twenties flee to Europe to drink themselves into oblivion, mostly under the café tables of Paris, but the majority of the serious writers stayed home and tackled the problems of life on the home ground. They adhered to a sort of intellectual "America Firstism" which set the task of analyzing, defining, and describing what was actually existent in America and what it meant. Even the ribald scorn of Henry Mencken attested to an intensity, even profundity, of interest in his country's manners, morals, and speech. He also was Americanist, and his hilarious revelations built up, in spite of his intentions perhaps, a mounting curiosity about the land and its ways of being and doing. Americans read him, and looked about to see if it was so.

The catastrophe of 1929, though it destroyed a lot of easy confidence in some circles, did not disrupt a strong belief among political thinkers and among the populace at large that there was an American way, in spite of the failure of the one just tried, which could lead us forward better than any way, radical or conservative, which postwar Europe had to offer. Even after ten years there was no faith in Europe's ability either to keep the peace or improve her politics or economy. Leftist solutions, such as those offered by the Russian Marxists and their followers, led to dictatorship, and no responsible American could look on that with tolerance. Rightist solutions were suspected because it appeared they led or might lead the same way. An intensive and vocal search for a new American way began as the twenties turned into the thirties. This was much less internationalist than the business way which preceded it. It was perhaps more genuinely "America First" through and through. It had no use for the disguised imperialisms of the international market and investment schools of big capital. Too many small Americans had been lately rooked in that game. It looked almost entirely to the home front for its inspiration and for the means to implement its American dream.

It had many facets. Some of these, as scared businessmen tried to adapt them, were obviously reactionary, chauvinistic, and devoted to the maintenance of special economic privileges, but by and large the new search for an American way pointed to the Left rather than the Right. It asked the question: "What about the Democracy we forgot to save?" and it answered: "Let's make it work at home." When the whole world began going down under the repercussions of the American business collapse, and millions were unemployed in our own country, the cry rose "Save America." As the international debacle increased, it rapidly became "Save America First." This new "America Firstism" was no mere jingoistic yap. It involved a deadly serious attempt to rebuild our society on democratic lines and to provide a wider and more stable distribution of the wealth which, for all the failures of business, was obviously still intact in our enormous resources.

The fact that the attempt had isolationist tendencies at times must not be permitted to disguise the other fact that it was pretty generaly liberal and humanitarian. The word *isolation*, we must also remember, represented an old historical American doctrine, which, though never tenable, had, as before noted, a great hold on the popular American mind. This doctrine had been greatly bolstered by the obvious failure of our First World War intervention to improve the international scene. Its regained strength in the late twenties and early thirties called up no ugly meanings. These came later when the Second World War began looming up. Admittedly the advocates of this reborn "America Firstism" did include men who later backed the Huey Long, Gerald K. Smith, Father Coughlin types of Neo-Fascism, but it also included a body of respectable and intellectually well-equipped political thinkers. Judge Jerome Frank, no narrow chauvinist and certainly no Fascist, could without misgiving even entitle a studious book *Save America First*. And Franklin Roosevelt in 1933, at the time of the famous World Economic Conference in London, could decide, to the consternation of the assembled international economists and bankers, that the problems of American economics came first, were primary to world ones, and must be settled on the home front first.

None of this liberalist "America Firstism" was ever crystallized into a political doctrine acceptable to all of its adherents. It couldn't be because of the multiplicity of its aspects and of its appeals. But it did call national attention to a reconsideration of American social purposes and to a redefining of the American way. As Roosevelt's administration, becoming the New Deal, began smashing into old and sacrosanct practices, this redefinition turned, as we all remember, into one of the bitterest political struggles of our history—and one not yet done with. On both sides of this battle, on the reformist as on the reactionary side, it is notable, however, that the effective appeal was largely to our own history, *not to a world image but to our own image*. A resuscitation occurred of the old eighteenth and early nineteenth century struggle about the nature of the society we intended. Were we a Republic or a Democracy?

A Democracy, said the adherents of labor and the poor farmer, the better part of the intellectuals, the Democratic party, and the President. A Republic, said most of the businessmen, the industrialists, the people of wealth, and what remained of the discredited Republican party. It was the old conflict, made new and loud and bitter. But it was an American conflict, and except for a small minority of Communists and their intellectual spokesmen, defined mostly in American terms. It reached such a climax in 1936 that every cocktail party or beerhall gathering ended in a fight.

Immensely affecting the more intelligent levels of this search for and struggle over the meaning of America were the new popularizations of American history by Charles and Mary Beard and James Truslow Adams which spotlighted for both sides the peculiar non-European character of our evolution. Other historical studies directly based on the Frontierism of Frederick J. Turner explored the dynamic energies and effects of our westward moving yesterday. Biographies, by the hundreds, dealing with American characters real and legendary flowed from the press. Our novelists, no matter how grim their pictures sometimes, painted them in vivid American colors. Carl Sandburg could turn even Chicago into a flaming symbol of American energy and drive. What were we, what are we, what do we intend to be, what can we be, *as Americans?* These were the questions.

Although this fervent national self-concentration was soon to be cut short by the rising totalitarianisms of Europe and Asia, it ruled the American mind during most of the thirties. In fact the whole interval, both in boom and depression, between our two great international involvments was an American interval—one which proclaimed the uniqueness of our civilization and its virtual independence of all others.

In the atmosphere this Americanism created, John Curry, Grant Wood, and I rose easily to our public acclaim and success. We were psychologically in tune with our time. We could hardly have avoided some kind of success.

In the artistic circles of New York, the Wood, Curry, Benton boom did not obtain the sanctions accorded it by the general public and the press. Nor did it win the approval of the wealthy minority over the country who collected pictures, especially modern French pictures. The museum trustees and their directors for the most part didn't like the looks of it either, although a few of the more venturesome made purchases. In the colleges and universities the professors of art, who like the critics were conditioned to a novel view of things by the Armory show of 1913 and the flood of literature on the "new aesthetics" which came out of Europe, shied off also. The "intellectuals," at least those rather self-consciously "high-brow" intellectuals who flirted with left-wing ideas and who wrote the elevated and brilliant commentaries in the little magazines, were decisively against it too.

There was a conglomerate of opinion, made up oddly, when it is examined, of what should have been mutually exclusive ideas, which set its face against the Wood, Curry, Benton "Regionalism." The same groups which looked suspiciously at me alone looked even more suspiciously at the three of us together. Although this animosity had many critical facets, it was sparked by two main lines of thought. One of these was political, the other aesthetic. These lines were often intertwined and so mixed up that the contradictions, above noticed, which they involved were obscured, and rich capitalists and their institutional front men often found themselves sitting in the same box with poor Communists and their intellectual spokesmen. For the sake of clarity, however, it is necessary to untangle these lines and treat them separately.

First, let me take up the political ideas which were directed against us.

In 1919, when, released from the Navy, I returned to New York and thought of painting again, the social divisions which I described a few pages back were getting well under way. There was much labor unrest, and there were many strikes. My first job was obtained by answering an advertisement in a New York paper which called for dock workers. I was dead broke and had to get money somehow. I worked as stevedore and then as cooper on the Hudson River piers. That I have told about in my autobiography. I neglected to tell, however, that after a couple of weeks on the job, I found out I was a "scab." I should have known this from the hundreds of idle men hanging out in the streets adjacent to the piers, but maybe because of my desperate need for cash, I didn't give it a thought until one noon in a side-street restaurant full of stevedores, I was questioned. It was laughingly done, and when I told my story of a busted ex-sailor—I still wore part of my Navy uniform—the Union boys told me to go on back to work. However, the business annoyed me, and after a few more days I quit.

Like most of the young artists and intellectuals who lived in New York just before the war, I had been touched by Socialist ideology. I knew the Fabians, mostly through Bernard Shaw, and I had read the *Communist Manifesto* and had had Karl Marx's *Das Kapital* explained to me. Although politically I was a conventional American Democrat, and voted that way when I took the trouble to vote at all, I entertained ideas about "capital and labor" much more radical than the Democratic party would have stood for. Thus no matter how much I needed money, I couldn't go on playing the "scab," even with what amounted to Union permission.

In the upheavals of the early twenties, during the Palmer raids and the crushings of the I.W.W., all of my sympathies were on the labor and radical side. So were those of every artist, every writer, and every intellectual I knew. When American participation in the League of Nations failed and the skullduggeries of its formation came to light under the reviews of the horrified "world imagists" and the more cynical but more immediately trenchant criticism of Woodrow Wilson's political enemies at home, it appeared that only some kind of world-wide socialism could bring man's life to a decent order. It seemed to those of us who tried to think in our poverty-stricken studios about what was happening around us that an entirely new world was due. Looking eastward, we thought we saw it in the making. Although I was never an actual member of any of the radical cliques and retained somewhat more skepticism than the better part of my radical friends—I was not given to over-all idealistic beliefs and had already been propelled by my Navy experience toward specifically Americanist views—I was pretty well on their side and with them applauded the success of Lenin and Trotsky in establishing what appeared to be a true socialist state.

This leaning was increased by reading. The literature most commonly circulated among my crowd was largely based on mid-nineteenth century determinism. Marxist doctrine in the political and economic field, as the last expression of that determinism, seemed logically irrefutable. Commentators on history, even our American Charles Beard in his *Economic Interpretation of the Constitution*, along with philosophers and legalists, were writing in terms which encouraged ideas of economic determinism in conformity at least with those of Karl Marx. The books of the learned, or near-learned, the "liberal" and "radical" magazines which we all read avidly, conditioned us to accept the premises of Marxism as absolutely sound.

Once these premises were accepted, a very simple logic could easily capture us and make us believe that Russian Communism, as the only practically operative form of Marxism, provided the most advanced form of society ever known and the most hopeful for mankind. Returning visitors who proclaimed the forward looking and liberal nature of the new Russian institutions re-enforced this. The actual decrees of the Lenin government also indicated that Utopian conditions were in the making in Russia which were in utter contrast to the repressive conditions obtaining in our own society. Even when the boom began alleviating such conditions in America, most of the people I associated with could see no reasons for moving away from the promises of Russian Communism. They could see no benefits in a Wall Street dominated society for themselves, and there weren't, or for the country at large.

Neither could I. The idea of a ruthless and greedy

crowd of economic buccaneers sucking the life blood of the country for their profits was familiar to me before I had ever heard of Karl Marx, Communism, or even Socialism. It was acceptable on plain American grounds. It had long been a part of Midwestern Democratic campaign talk, and I could remember it from my earliest childhood. My father was always quoting our old Missouri Senator George Vest's famous description of the cow "which had its head in the west where it ate, and its teats in Wall Street where it was milked." I had been raised on the idea that the big capitalist monopolies, centered in New York, were against the "people's" interests; and Russian moves toward a "people's" control of these, or what purported to be such, seemed to me eminently desirable.

When I first started painting my American Histories, 1919 to 1924, I could see no conflict between American democratic ideals and the ideals of Soviet Russia. My readings in American history were convincing me that the "people" of America—the simple, hard working, hard fighting people who had poured out over the frontiers and built up the country—were, more often than not, deprived of the fruits of their labors by combinations of politicians and big businessmen. I was convinced that the American dream had been continually discounted by capitalist organizations which had grown beyond the people's control. All of this kept me in substantial agreement with those Marxist historians and political theorists who were describing America in Marxist terms. As late as 1931, I could illustrate a book for one of these, Leo Hubermann's *We the People*, and feel in intellectual harmony with its writer.

However, I had begun having misgivings about the Marxist view of things as early as 1926. My trips over the country were giving me a "feel" of America and suggesting that the Marxist pattern of economic determination, determination by productive instrumentalities, was not alone sufficient to describe all the forces at work in our society, either presently or historically. Also I was being stumped by the Marxist picture of history as a "dialectic" progression. It was too obvious that this picture was an intellectual feat, a "tour de force" which tried to give a rational grammatic pattern to what my mounting experience told me could not be wholly rationalized. I had by this time also begun reading John Dewey. Although it took me several years to dig through the Dewey language, his attitudes toward the "question of certitude," so different from Marx's, was making a strong impression. I was by temperament very skeptical of intellectual summaries anyhow, and particularly with regard to history which I could see was very largely written under logical requirements, that is under the necessity of making *chains* of events. As different historians made different chains, it was hard to tell which was a "true" one. This problem, essentially of the relation of "form" to "reality," was already well known to me. In the concrete instances of my own art I faced it every day. Any logical form I knew, even when it appeared adequately representative of what was *real*, had to be partially fictitious. Life was not logical. Reality, in its totality, was too varied to be formally contained.

Nevertheless it was not until the early thirties, when the breakdown of "Business First" re-stimulated all the radical and reformist forces of America and revolutionary doctrines of all kinds struggled again to get a foothold in the *practical* world, that I broke with my Marxist friends. Up till then in spite of some differences, which I kept more or less secret because I was not sure of my ground, I was on reasonably good terms with the boys of the John Reed Club and the Russo-American front in general. The "boys" did not begin calling me a reactionary, "nationalist reactionary," traitor, and chauvinist until later.

Looking back it is easy to see how they came to do so. I had generally agreed with them about the repressions of the early twenties and with their criticisms of the "Business First" society of boom days, whose energies, though I admired them as an American spectacle, were obviously concentrating the wealth of the country in the hands of nonproductive speculators. A brokers' heyday didn't spell out the American dream. I had agreed also, admittedly with some naïveté as to definition, that what was needed for "peace and progress" was a "people's society," one where the people, that is, would have control over the instruments of production. "Industrial as well as political democracy" was, and still is for that matter, a tenet I believed in. I was pro-labor, anti-big capitalist, and psychologically ready for large-scale social change.

When I began turning away from the intellectual rigidities of Leninist-Marxist patterns, it was natural that those who adhered to them and believed wholeheartedly in the specific lines of social action they proposed should see me as a renegade and an enemy of all progressivism, just as later they saw Max Eastman, Sidney Hook, and others who, on more learned grounds than mine, also turned away. The Marxism of the artistic crowd of New York, and largely of the intellectual crowd also, was more an emotional allegiance than one of reason. It was a sort of passionate devotion to a salvation complex. By the opening of the thirties when Marxism-Leninism had taken on full-sounding religious overtones and had become an "orthodox" doctrine, it was impossible to question it, even slightly, without arousing religious emotions.

But as my reading, most of it, curiously enough, inspired by Communist pamphlets, was getting me more familiar with the philosophic origins of Marxism, there were questions. And very difficult ones. These, at least on their philosophic side, have no place in this writing, but they led me to a series of immediately practical questions about the "dictatorship of the proletariat" as an instrument to promote democracy either industrially or politically. I was enough of a politician by memories of family experience to know, and know with certitude, that governing power could not be exercised by the mass of the people, but that it had to be delegated to representatives. Mere mob power could not sustain itself as governing power. If the people, I asked, delegated their mass power with absolute completeness to a small convinced minority who, as Lenin posited, knew "What was good for the people," how could we be sure that that was going to result in anything different from all the well-known tyrannies of past history run by other minorities who also knew what was "good for people"? How did we know that Communist "ideals," "ideals of good for the people," would not come to be identified with what was "good" only for those who held power? Other "ideals" had time and again, and some of them only lately, turned sour under *knowing* guidance. The more I thought about dictatorship, the less I liked it, the less I believed in it, and the more certain I became that an alternative had to be found for it if any kind of dependable "good for the people" was to arrive.

All that was true in the Marxist picture of capitalist society, and I still agreed there was a great deal, all that was hopeful in its promise to reorganize the productive relations of society in favor of a larger common share was to my American mind, now pretty well filled with Americanist visions, largely invalidated by its grounding in dictatorship. I had seen too much of Bossism in our own American cities to have any faith in an intellectually or idealistically supported counterpart. I could see how Bossism worked in local places—how where it provided good, and it had at times, it demanded a price which was far from good. Would a national or international Bossism work better? I couldn't make myself believe it could. In the philosophic field I had learned of the German Hegel's identification of the "theoretical good" with the Prussian monarchy whose last boss, Kaiser Wilhelm, had left little good for anybody in Europe, least in the end for the very people to whom he promised the most of it. I suspected that Marx's inversion of Hegel's "dialectical system," which put the "theoretic good" in a new Bossism, left similar possibilities.

All of this seems trite as I go over it today, but it was not so in New York circles of the late twenties and early thirties. Stalinist nationalism had not risen to the point where the real hand of the new Russia was evident. In 1928 even John Dewey could come back from Moscow with a glowing account of the "progress" of Communism. What I had to say, even tentatively, looked like "black reaction" to nearly everybody in New York's radical and progressive circles.

My refusal in the winter of 1928-29 to enlist my art in the "Marxist social propaganda" advocated by the Mexican revolutionary artist Diego Rivera and dear to the boys of the Communist John Reed Club, added to this blackness. Later in a talk before the members of this Club where I tried to explain that my art was dedicated to a realistic representation of the American people and to the American social scene *as it was* rather than to propagating ideas about how it *should be*, I was hooted down. When I said that "realism" could not be defined as socialist or capitalist, but had to rest on the "real" that one experienced directly and that the John Reed Club artists couldn't paint anything *real* about America because their European-derived Communist preconceptions wouldn't permit real experiences of American situations, an enraged Commie threw a chair at me and turned the meeting into a yelling shambles. Things were pretty hot.

As enmities rose and I found myself continuously on the defensive, I began saying outright that Communism was nothing but a new oriental religion and that its authoritative structure could only be put over on people who, like the Russians, had been raised in an authoritarian society and had never had a chance to think democratically in their politics. Although I applauded the new Mexican revolutionary art because of its grounding in the actualities of Mexican life and thought, rather than in Parisian aesthetics, I said that it could not be taken as a model for the art of our northern civilization because that had had a different kind of life and thought.

I said that as Mexican history, like that of Russia, had been largely a history of dictatorships and authoritarian religious institutions, it was understandable that Mexicans like Orozco, Siqueiros, and Rivera would think in the terms of an authoritative social theory like Marxism, but that it was foolish for us in the United States, with our long experience of divided political powers and divided religious institutions, to try to see eye to eye with them. This was perhaps a little loose in view of the history of Mexican philosophical and political thought but not nearly so loose as what was being thrown at me by those who were imitating the forms of Mexican revolutionary propaganda. With regard to these latter, I insisted that Mexican forms, which, no matter what their idealistic content, actually represented Mexican cultural conditions, were not transferable to other cultural conditions. Because of this I held it was just as hopeless to try to make North American art by imitating Mexicans as it was by imitating Frenchmen.

I was not, as I have said, opposed to the Mexican art. I was, in fact, at the very time of my refusal to enter its propagandist front an associate and close friend of Clemente Orozco in a New York gallery venture which starred the two of us. He had as little use for his New York imitators as I had and realized as thoroughly as I that the differences in our cultural backgrounds called for different kinds of art. Orozco had plenty of prejudices, and thoroughly well justified ones, against the United States, but he never carried these over into a criticism of my attempts to picture the country. It was, as a matter of fact, these very attempts which originally led to our association. Orozco never quite attached himself to the propagandist views of Rivera. He did not believe that painting was a vehicle for verbal messages. In that we were in agreement.

At the end of 1932, when the unveiling of the Whitney Museum mural loosed a new storm of left-wing criticism of my work and my retaliatory blood got up, I said, with something less than tact, that the trouble with all New York radicalism was that it was dominated by people whose American backgrounds were of too recent an origin to permit them to know or understand America. Further, I said that if these new Americans wanted to affect social changes in America, and were not just blabbing, that they had better study the history of American political thought, which was not, I emphasized, when seen realistically and with a knowledge of the social conditions it represented, the mere capitalist fraud the Marxists took it to be. This was, of course, ultimate heresy. It hit at sacrosanct Marxist assumptions of realism as well as at the American inapplicability of Marxist political techniques.

Now a good many of my pronouncements at this time were made in heat and often, as I have before related, with the help of bootleg hooch which was not notable for its moderating influence. Pretty soon I found myself tagged with "antiforeignism" and made into a sort of spokesman for the Hearstites and the Chicago Tribunites and other dubious Americanists, including even the Klu Kluxers, remnants of which still survived the scandals of the early twenties. Because there were many young Jews, as was inevitable in New York, attached to the city's Marxist groups, it was easy to give my growing anti-Marxism an anti-Semitic cast. The "'Commies" had already learned the technique of the smear.

In this way, the stage was set for my left-wing role of the middle and late thirties as a Fascist, jingoist, anti-Semitic, and reactionary son-of-a-bitch. So deeply had Marxist views penetrated into intellectual circles, even into aesthetic circles, which, as I shall later show, really represented something utterly different from Marxism, that the "intellegentsia" as a whole regarded my left-wing role as a true one.

As Grant Wood and John Curry became more and more publicly associated with me, they were given roles similar to mine. Although neither Wood nor Curry had consorted with Marxist groups or publicly quarreled with them and although they were almost completely non-political, they were stained with my colors, and the Americanist movement we initiated as a trio became as chauvinist and reactionary as I was supposed to be. This was carried over to the few critics who dared approve us and, in truth, to all who associated with us.

When I began answering criticisms of our joint movement with the same smear techniques accorded it, animosity was so generally intensified that old Fred Price, whose Feragil Galleries on Fifty-seventh Street gave our regionalism its New York showings, came to me and said "Tom, for God's sake, shut up. You are not only making the 'Commies' mad, you are making everybody mad." He was seconded by Curry, who was extremely sensitive to criticism and who thought that argument did us more harm than good.

But it was hard for me to keep myself in hand. One highball and one newspaper man, and I was off. Years later, looking back over these days, Reginald Marsh said: "It was Tom Benton who made the enemies of American Realism." He meant it was my "loud mouth," I guess.

Now on the aesthetic side, opposition to our Americanist Regionalism, if not as violent or as given to personal smearing, was just as fervent as it was on the Marxist side. This opposition was also "internationalist" in its coloration, though it depended for its ideology on movements which had grown up and were culturally localized in the Montparnasse and Montmarte quarters of Paris. Not so clearly defined, and with none of the logical justifications of Marxism, it provided nevertheless even better critical tools with which to operate on our American localism. It cut where this could really hurt, in the area of the pocketbook. Its appeal was not merely to a group of poverty-stricken radical artists, political-minded intellectuals, or uneasy critics, but to the wealthy people who bought pictures, financed collections, filled the museum trusteeships, and gave endowments to the colleges and universities. It appealed to the old distrust, which wealthy and cultivated Americans, along with so many American intellectuals, always seem to have of the possibilities of their own culture.

This distrust has no relation to the liberalist criticisms of our institutions, noted a few pages back, or with any thoughts of reorganizing the production relations of our society in the interests of the American dream. By no means. It is simply a form of colonialism which feels that identification of some sort with an older mother culture gives a superior status in a new one. It reflects a kind of shame of the real and actual. The meat packer who has become a millionaire is no longer just a butcher when his house is full of great cultural imports. These give him an aristocratic air which the real facts of his life would hardly accord. The wife of the advertising magnate can rise above the vulgarities of her husband's trade and live in a compensatory world when her living room is full of elegantly framed and puzzling French pictures. She can assert with confidence her superiority to the life she actually lives by. A somewhat similar thing goes for the more sterile types among the intellectuals, for the "high-brows" who compensate for their lack of creative ability at home by living vicariously in a distant creativeness. In other places I have told how this cultural distrustfulness impelled the American artist to attach himself to European aesthetic movements in order to acquire the trappings of artistic status.

For a while in the late thirties, when our Americanist Regionalism was in full swing and the programs of the Federal Government were calling attention to the aesthetic possibilities of the American environment, I had a feeling that perhaps a permanent dent had been made in all this colonialism. Some dent was effected, as the continuing sales of my own pictures indicated, but not enough to hold American art on tracks of its own. As I write now, painting movements, aesthetic attitudes in the colleges, and critical rationalizations in the press, along with collectors' interests, are even more tied to Parisian turn-of-the-century thinking than they were before Wood, Curry, and I came to our

Americanist positions. Our influence on the young is negligible. An imported "aesthetic" is, at least for the moment, again very generally a mere imitative manifestation in America.

What is the Parisian developed "Modernism" which is so persistently effective on the American artistic mind? Is it the universally valid movement its protagonists claim it to be? Let's look at this second question. The answer is "Yes" if the artistic culture of Paris is taken to be a universal culture and the aesthetic techniques used to express the conditions of that culture are taken to be universally applicable. Otherwise the answer would seem to be "No." How can aesthetic affirmations arising from the particular conditions of one environment be applicable to other and different conditions?

At first glance it would seem that they couldn't, but there arises here a peculiar phenomenon of the modern world which complicates matters. In this world, and especially from about 1850 on, the only artistic affirmations made at all were largely confined to Paris. A few lonely painters, a few sculptors arose here and there, even in the Americas, but they worked generally without much recognition. In the great industrialisms and exploitative imperialisms of "laissez faire" capitalism which prevailed in the world from 1850 to 1914 there arose no conditions which really called for or even seemed to permit aesthetic representation. At least there were none to much encourage such representation. As a consequence of this, artistic-minded people from all over flocked to Paris and identified themselves with Parisian cultural conditions and imitated its expressions. In a sense they thus universalized these because when they returned home, they took them along.

How was it that Paris, the chief city of a country as capitalist-minded and as money-mad as any other during the heyday of free capitalist "individualistic" enterprise, the very native home in fact of money-minded bourgeoisism— how was it that she could maintain an atmosphere conducive to aesthetic endeavor while no other city was able to? The answer to this seems to lie very largely in the fact that long before the capitalist world had risen, Art had been given a special place in Parisian life. It had been separated from

French cultural conditions in their totality and transferred to special conditions maintained almost wholly in and about Paris. This isolation of art from the generality of French culture had begun in the fifteenth and sixteenth centuries when, by kingly edict, Italianate Renaissance artistic cultures supplanted the indigenous French Gothic ones. Art became then a special *extra-cultural* manifestation existing apart from a total culture. It made its chief appeal to a small minority of aristocratic elegants. In this new, and generally highly eclectic form, it nevertheless turned eighteenth century Paris into the aesthetic capital of Europe.

During the Monarchy, Parisian art functioned in spite of its limited place in society. It reflected an aristocratic dream-world. It built up a charming panorama of gay pretenses to reflect like pretenses in the social group which supported it. Within that group it was exceedingly popular, and it turned their city of Paris itself into a work of art, with a most elegant façade.

After the Revolution the art of the French aristocracy was left hanging in the air so far as functional purpose was concerned. The rich French bourgeois manufacturer or industrialist of the nineteenth century might purchase it as an item of display, but it could only represent his wealth, not himself or the real life he lived. Art became thus a form of exhibitionism. It served to exhibit moneyed status; it helped wealth to appear as aristocratic as was the real aristocracy of yesterday. The rich French bourgeois had always envied and worshiped that aristocracy, and when he came to power, he imitated it. Art was one of its trappings, so he encouraged art whether or not he understood it. In the seesaws of empire and republic, he kept for it an official status. It exhibited not only his own personal superiority, but maintained the old eighteenth century superiority of his city of Paris in matters of elegance, fashion, and civilized manner. In the rising capitalist world, this was a practical matter which good French businessmen well understood. The new aristocracy of the industrial world had to purchase its cultural trappings. Paris would supply them.

Exhibitions of cultural goods, inclusive of the goods of "high" art, became a Parisian nineteenth century tradition. The salons where art was exhibited became internationally famous. In these salons the personal exhibition-ism which proclaimed new wealth was transferred to the creative processes of art. The artist himself became an ex-hibitionist striving always for new effects which would manifest the uniqueness of his personal vision and make him stand out an individual in a world of competing in-dividuals. Most of the art of the salons was pretentious, empty, an art of gestures and "recherché" meanings, pseudo-classic, romantic, grandiose, and plainly symbolic of the new millionairism of the day which sought to cover its origins with the garments of dream. As it was the mecca of aristocratic elegants in the eighteenth century, Paris was now the mecca of the moneyed elegants of the new bourgeois world.

The high period of free capitalist enterprise, of in-dividualistic "public be damned" commercial and industrial self-assertiveness, ran through the 1870's and 1880's up to 1914. This was the great time of the doctrine of "laissez faire." Paris, the cultural capital of the Western World and the chief caterer to its parvenues, permitted "laissez fairism" a complete, full, and profitable development. The Parisians were logical: a free world meant a wholly free one, one released from all conformity, inclusive of moral con-formity. Short of outright murder, an individual with money, of course, could do and think as he pleased in Paris as the nineteenth century went into the twentieth. Sex in all its manifestations was unfettered. Men, women, and children put their various charms publicly on sale. Any individual who could get a stage of any sort, and who could put on any sort of original or unique act, was certain of acclaim. When an aging President of the Republic died in an unfortunate position next to a lady of fashion, he drew nothing but admiring exclamations from the whole Parisian populace. They loved his senile audacity. In pre-World War days, Paris was probably freer than any city in the world had even been. There were no compulsions. It was a wonderful place. I was there.

In this atmosphere modern art was born to express aesthetically and for the first time in history the ultimate and final anarchic right of the individual soul—released from all scruple, all social responsibility, and all the ancient canons of Western life and thought and form—to assert itself, exhibit itself before the world, and proclaim its uniqueness. The blade of grass found itself and marvelled and spoke out loud.

But other blades growing beyond the purlieus of Parisian art were not always aware of the uniqueness of this artistic blade, or if aware they were indifferent to it. They had their own individual concerns and their own "rights of the soul" which were just as real when directed to getting money or power or women as when set to making art. The grass roots of the great world of active men and women were not intertwined with those which shot up the new blades of art. Even in Paris, which would applaud almost anything and where Art was a cultural fetish and a good advertisement of the city's cultural superiority, it was a social oddity, something apart. Although it might and sometimes did reflect the conditions of society, it arose through no demands by society. It could function in the capitalist mores of society only as a commercial product, as a picture-dealer's item in a competitive money game. The serious artist—and in spite of the above pictured hoopla environment which produced the modern artist, there were some—was forced to build a public if he was to have one at all. There was no unified cultural body as in the days of the eighteenth century monarchy to which his work might have a logical attachment.

This became more and more true as art moved into the twentieth century. Even the polite and charming French bourgeoisism of moderate wealth to which the painter Renoir had attached himself at the end of the nineteenth century, and of which his art was so largely expressive, was passing. The mass production machine age drive of the new century was destroying its old "franc in the stocking" independence and its functioning place in society. The day of the big capitalist combines, though it was not recognized in the individualistic behaviors and beliefs prevailing, had come.

Between 1908 and 1914 the artist began erecting cults to sustain himself. He tried to harmonize these with the growing scientifically-directed machine world. To the credit of his intuition, let me say here, he sensed his losing position, his real and accelerating uselessness in society.

But he tried to remedy this by an intellectual make-believe. He proclaimed himself a sort of aesthetic scientist who worked in his studio as a physical scientist worked in his laboratory. In the place of facts he was to discover new aesthetic modes, new ways and means, and new values. He was an experimenter in the world of sensations, he said, and his business was to help others experience the deep and profound wonders he found there. Unfortunately these wonders were not checkable or measurable in any true scientific sense. They had to be accepted as revelations—on faith. Each artist working alone in his studio laboratory became thus a sort of prophet. He cried out in a wilderness of aesthetically indifferent, backward and unprogressive philistines. Many prophets and many cults arose. They were all substantially alike. And in like manner, they all called out to the damned. Those who recognized their prophecies were saved, released from their philistinism, and put in the company of the elect.

The twentieth century sons and daughters, especially the daughters, of the old nineteenth century millionaires, ashamed of the now obviously fraudulent nature of their fathers' aristocratic pretenses, flocked to these cults in droves. Satiated with money, travel, parties, the whole materialistic world of new wealth, here was an adventure to undertake, an adventure of the soul. Daughters often aging a little and past the time when they might suggest other than soulful adventures, especially American daughters of oil, copper, soap, steel, toilet paper, or what not, suddenly realized that they were really deeply sensitive human beings and that a way had been found to manifest the fact. The cults of Paris, and peripheral ones which grew in their likeness in New York, thrived. Shrewd dealers took them up. Little galleries, shaded, softened, attended by pretty and impeccably groomed young men, called to the newly elect. Before handsomely framed smears of color, the daughters swooned. "How wonderful to know about art and see at last that money means so little in our real lives," they said. "How true," said the pretty young salesmen. "Give it to us."

Although modern or what we now call "modernist" art is mainly a child of the highly idiosyncratic individualism promoted by the Parisian bohemians of this century, a sort of last frenzied call of a dying era, it has a rational history. It is not just crazy self-assertion alone. Back of the gesturing official salons of mid-nineteenth century Paris, participating in them but with difficulty and always belatedly, was a surge of genuine Gallic creativeness more distinctive than any which had occurred since Gothic days, more truly French. Although this surge was, like the official art of the academies and salons, without deep roots in French life as a whole and by no means, as noted, the outcome of any calls from that life, it did somehow achieve a connection with it. A group of painters, the Barbizon school, went to the French land, and came out with a new naturalism. A great artist, Courbet, with his eyes glued to life, came up with a new realism. Although this was technically Dutch and Spanish inspired, its concentration on French life and its new visualism overshadowed this. Modern art began with Courbet. Not with Delacroix, as is so often assumed, but with Courbet. Delacroix was technically tied to the Renaissance, to Rubens and the Venetians and to the great European formal traditions. Courbet made the first clear break with these. Following him through Manet to the Impressionists proper—Monet, Pissarro, Sisley, and Renoir —art broke more and more with its ancient European disciplines. There were exceptions, like the great graphic art of Daumier, but generally the new tendencies initiated by the Barbizon painters and forcefully emphasized by Courbet ignored old compositional methods in favor of a new one.

Although I have not space here fully to explore this new composition, it was notably affected by Daguerre's lately invented photographic processes which brought visual nature to a flat plane directly and without any dependence on organizational techniques. We today have forgotten how revolutionary an invention photography was and how marvelous it seemed at its inception and how much it affected ideas of the visual world. However, to anyone who looks with an open eye at the painting which preceded photography and that which followed it the influence of photographic vision is obvious. The old organization of parts in a geometric scheme, first in two and then in three dimensions, which was characteristic of Western painting from the Ravenna mosaics up to the middle of the nineteenth century, is supplanted by a direct visualism. This visualism is not representative of the normal processes of human *seeing*, which is a complex of funded experiences of all sorts, but is rather a derivative of the mechanical processes initiated by photography. Before the coming of a successful photography, such visualism was conceivable, but not realizable. I do not mean to say here that the human mind did not operate in painting after photography arose. I mean only that in the special techniques of composition it tended to operate differently.

The art of the French Impressionists, though it developed a novel quasi-scientific pigmental process, is almost pure visualism. It was grounded in "sensation" or what purported to be so. Pure sensations, if there be any, are, of course, highly private and by themselves *provide no meanings*. Actually they can be registered only by machines. Nevertheless, "Sensationalism" was the watchword of Impressionism. It meant the cultivation of a personal, private, individual response to the "facts" of nature, primarily a visual response, as in the famous haystacks of Monet painted at different times of the day to show different light conditions. With this "sensationalism," meaningless itself, went a repudiation of the value of all meaning for painting, and of the significance of subject matter which suggested meaningful ideas. As one American critic aptly put it, apples were equalized with Madonnas. As being less humanly suggestive, apples and their abstract equivalents even took the place of Madonnas when modern art became the "modernistic" art of the twentieth century.

But as soon as Impressionism began to be adopted by the outside world, which looked to Paris for examples to copy, it was attacked from the inside. The most famous French artist of modern times, and in some ways the most interesting of all French artists, saw that the new visualism of Impressionism was leading to chaos. Paul Cézanne turned his thought back to the great forms of the past. He realized that, for all its lively color, Impressionism was formless, that it lacked substance, power, and even the "reality" it purported to represent. Decidedly of his time, however, he clung to what he called his "little sensations," to his private responses to the simple *being* of things in nature—not to their place in a scale of human meanings, but to their bare existence. "A pictorial truth exists in objects," he said.

He clung also to the Impressionist "color vibrancies" which had come to represent the "truth of nature." When he said "we can never be too submissive" to nature, he meant Impressionist "nature," the nature of color sensation. He is explicitly clear on this point. "One must return to classicism, but through *nature*, that is to say through *sensation*" is one of his famous remarks. Another, "I imagine Poussin entirely repainted after *nature*, that is the classic I understand."

He set out to reconstruct his world of nature, to represent his "little sensation" in the terms of classic geometric structure, but by means of color. His new geometry would be one of color planes. He wanted to make Impressionism, nature through color, "as solid and durable as the art of the galleries," that is to say, as the great European art of the past.

Paul Cézanne was, as I have said, an exceedingly interesting figure. At a time when artists were dealing with *effects*, he tackled the fundamentals of the creative processes in painting. He pointed up, as no man ever had before, the central problem of painting, the old perhaps insoluble problem of the relation of form, which is a matter of knowledge, to color, which is a matter of sensational impact. His actual solutions, when compared to others made before him, are not, as time goes by, as tremendous as his disciples believed, but they laid bare and emphasized the issues. Perhaps the very inadequacy of his ideas helped in this matter. His concepts were full of contradictions. He would "represent nature by means of the cylinder, the sphere, the cone, *all placed in perspective*," but he must not obey "the logic of the mind," only "the *logic* of his eyes," of his sensations— of his color sensations. Out of his struggles with the *known* solid world and the directly *felt* world of sensation were born all the technical precedents of "modernism." Also out of his highly individualistic attitude—he dreamed of being a "sensitive plate," oblivious of all save his reactions (note the odd reference to the camera)—came a good part of the sanctions for the sensibility-cultivating individualisms of our own day. Not all of them, but a good part.

Others than Cézanne made their impact on late nine-teenth century French art—Gauguin, Van Gogh, Renoir, and a host of lesser individualists—but the chain from Courbet to our day is maintained chiefly by Cézanne. Another chain, not quite so well appreciated at the moment and hidden somewhat by Cézanne's inheritance of the flattening visualisms of photography and Impressionism, is the chain he tied to the Renaissance and to the three-dimensional techniques of that period. "Nature exists in depth more than in the surface," he said.

Cézanne, for all his curious contradictions, had what the other artists of his time did not, a good mind and one able to make quite deep penetrations. Van Gogh, his next in influence, especially in Germanic circles, turned Impressionism into a very non-Gallic expressionism, into a typically northern form of soul exhibitionism. Van Gogh "expressed his emotions" and did his full part in setting up the final modernist conditions which I shall describe a little later. But he was not the source of much technical inspiration. He was a little too much of an individualist.

Cézanne had a universality of appeal. His philosophy and his art, though tied most emphatically to his own highly personal reactions, nevertheless carried universally valid ideas. Although Cézanne was as French as French can be and was an intensely poetic lover of his native locale —"There is a sadness in Provence that no one yet has sung," he cries—his thoughts had value for people all over the world. He could live narrowly and never for long away from a familiar home environment and yet be of a universal significance. Perhaps it was because of the very narrowness of his human life that Cézanne was able to concentrate the attention necessary to reach at universal meanings. As a provincial small towner of the South of France, which he always remained, he escaped the smug and superficial intellectualisms of the Parisian sophisticates. Away from the disturbing effects of clever urban pretense, he was able to probe seriously.

It is difficult to assess Cézanne's mind because it has become a sort of myth to which people attach what they please in the way of meaning. In spite of a constant revelation of depth, the naïveté and illogical nature of his pronouncements is, as I have noted, confusing. His central thought is hard to get at. The father of so many teachers is no clear teacher himself. He seems certainly to have believed that the "reality" of life, "nature" in his usual way of speaking, was a thing existing apart from himself which had to be *discovered* through a direct sensuous searching. Apparently he did not believe it was simply *given* without the need of effort. He insists that what is "real" is not easy to find, not easy to "realize." But in finding or "realizing" the "real," the senses, he indicates, are most dependable. The power of realization comes by sheer sense penetration. There is an almost oriental savor in the way he continually places this kind of intuition above the "logic of the mind." But although it contradicts in a way his own very Western constructive logic, his technical concern with the conjunctions of geometric solids, it is basically significant. It is especially so in view of what occurred later under the influence of his constructionist techniques. It is to be noted that he was concentrating on a "reality" or "nature" which existed, as I said above, beyond himself and which had to be "submitted" to before it could be grasped. In analysis this comes up to a very common-sense view of "reality," to an everyday picture of nature. And so it is. Cézanne was not an idealist. Nor was he any other kind of philosophic introvert. For all his talk about his "little sensation" and the intense turning in on the self it seems to imply, it is plain that he cherished it not for itself, but for what it revealed about something else. Neither was Cézanne an aesthetic hedonist to live on a mere titillation of the senses. He was obviously concerned with a *public* nature. Nowhere does he assume nature to be a *property* of his perceptions. She is out there. "I," he complains, "have not the magnificent coloring that makes *nature* live." Nature has the "real" coloring. She it is who makes the "little sensation" a thing of significance.

"You Americans are too literal when looking at paintings. Only the painting is important, the subject is nothing."

This remark, with its none too subtle priggishness, was made by a fashionable "modernist" painter of Paris, visiting America at the time of this writing. It serves well to introduce what ensued in Parisian art when Cézanne died. As will be seen, no opportunities for literal interpretation were offered in the new developments—none whatever.

Cézanne's technical experiments, his studies of formalizing method, of the problems of ways and means, were separated by his twentieth century disciples from their subject "nature" and made to stand apart. Their purpose was changed from the "realization" of experiences had in an outside world to the expression of subjective ones in the artist's private mind. In this way the motives for art, wholly located in the isolated interior soul, lost all public value, became in fact "as nothing." The "little sensation" turned into the more subjective "little emotion" which could be satisfactorily felt without any studied investigation of what made it occur. The "little sensation," although it was a private matter, presumed something outside the self; the "little emotion" was wholly inside—any hallucination could occasion it, any swelling of the ego instigate its exhibition. All paintings and sculpture in the new verbiage elicited by art's change of character became an expression of "aesthetic emotions." The artists of Paris, a good lot of them now bohemian expatriates, tied to nothing save their own egos, pitiful wanderers, so many on the outskirts of life, ceased thinking at all about concrete matters, such as those of Cézanne's "nature" which, as I have emphasized, existed in a public stream beyond himself, and turned completely to the "aesthetic emotions" which resided in their creative acts. The picture or the carving did then become all important. Mere combinations of color and shape, disconnected from all serious reference to a publicly apprehensible subject matter, ruled the exhibition halls.

Again this new turn, however, was not utterly empty or without any semblance of reason. It did reaffirm—what had been largely lost in a society devoted to the curious *abstractions* of a money profit way of life—that some values, and quite important ones, *did* exist in purely sensuous existences. It said that color, line, shape—the main properties of the visible world—were good in themselves if they were really tasted. They are. It said, further, that these properties were not necessarily tied to a mere *visualistic* experience, that they were not merely elements of a momentary visual sensation, but could be abstracted and used to represent concepts of the human mind. They can. And it was always assumed, before the days of Impressionism and photography, that they could. Nevertheless, after Impressionism, this reaffirmation of an old truth was of some value. In addition, the new movements, though with a very imperfect logic, stressed the psychologic fact that the world we human beings know is mostly the outcome of our own human perceptual constructions and that it, very possibly, has no ultimately testable reality.

This idealistic and very un-Cézannesque touch did hit a basic philosophic problem and did point up the highly plural nature of reality as an actual fact in human life. By referring to primitive constructions, to the symbolic arts of societies long dead, the modernists helped us to understand better that the *seen* world and what is taken to be the *real* world have been sometimes far apart, and for good practical reasons. They helped thereby, though as yet somewhat unsuccessfully, to replace photographic visualism as a true representation of the real with the old perceptual *inner seeing* on which the reality of art was based in its great historic periods. However, for all that was good in this modernism, from a nearly philosophic and from a strictly technical point of view—many technical procedures were drawn from primitivism which, especially in the combination with Western classic technique, have not yet been fully explored—the movement as a whole failed to come up with clearly stated definitions or with a clearly defined path for development. It was too personal, too individualistic, too egocentric to get out of the realm of a loose form of "genius" exhibitionism. The meanings of its art, when any were actually arrived at, were very largely limited to process. When even this became too rigorous, and it did, meaning became a matter of pure personal whimsy. In its last phase, meaning of any sort, even that of a mere decorative arrangement, even that of the most private "little emotion," was discarded. Modern art became, especially in its American derivations, a simple smearing and pouring of material, good for nothing but to release neurotic tensions. Here finally it became like a bowel movement or a vomiting spell.

So, even in its technical development from Cézanne until today, art paralleled the course it took as a social phenomenon, the course described a few pages back, which ended in a private soul cultism. Separated from a publicly meaningful subject, from ideas, legends, stories, religious or secular, and then from the concrete factors of a public nature, it sustained itself by a compensatory make-believe. The anarchic individualisms of modern art are today expressive of nothing whatever in the going forces of society. Individualism, except as the illusory hangover of a few privileged money groups, died with the First World War. It is no more a cultural fact of significance. The ultraindividualistic expressions of modernist art now prevailing, though they go under the name of an "Avant-garde," are thus cultural lags. They express what is forever dead, perhaps what never really lived except in the last frenzied cry of a city which sensed the coming of the end of its greatness, its power and its glory.

The "make-believes," which I have shown to be at the heart of modernism, parallel the make-believe states of mind which prevail in large sections of the business world of our own country. These same "make-believes" are prominently evident in the rather certainly decaying capitalist societies of Europe. They are particularly characteristic of those of France. The privatism of modernism, its grounding in an exaggerated individualism, goes along with the social privatism which can be sustained today only by a few people whose capital permits them to live above the real compulsions of society.

The obscurantist routines of modernist art, like the pretentious and empty routines of that functionless uppercrust of capitalist society, with its accompanying crust of uneasy high-brows, which as I have said lives largely by illusion, are best protected when they avoid the "vulgarities" of a common-sense realistic or popular point of view.

There have been some interesting pictures, I must admit, even distinguished ones, which have come out of modernist experiment. Talent is always around and manages to show itself even under the most adverse conditions. Most of these modernist pictures, however, have come out of France and are the result, as I have indicated, of a peculiarly French technical and social development. This development was *universalized* only because of default in other countries. It was adopted to fill a state of aesthetic emptiness or what appeared to be so. It has failed. This is particularly true in the case of the United States where art exhibitions, one after the other, proclaim only the most slavish imitations of French models. A few, a very few, American modernist artists have managed to inject a personal point of view into their works. Even these, however, have followed in the psychological path set by the artists of Paris and make exceedingly exclusive appeals. They express and depend upon a protected and specially cultivated élite which is out of touch with most of that which is real in our American life.

Now art may be and has been all through history collected and acclaimed by specially privileged groups, living above society as a whole. These have admittedly performed a socially useful function in preserving the world's great art. They have set up the great collections and built up the museums where the aesthetic history of man can be seen in all its concrete manifestations. These groups are, however, rarely creative. Not many, like the aristocrats of monarchical Paris, have helped to make an art in their image. For the most part they worship the past—even the ancient Roman upper classes did so—and imitations of the past or, like the French King Francis I, imports from cultures other than their own. The United States, having no aesthetic past, follows naturally in the path of Francis. The cultural import stands for Art. Imitations of these stand for a living art.

Along with the concrete import itself—the work of art—come also the attitudes of mind which occasioned it. These are rarely adaptable. They result in such concoctions as those of the seventeenth century French painter LeBrun where Italianate attitudes of the high Renaissance were forcibly thrust into French decoration. Only after these attitudes were thoroughly Gallicized did they become fruitful and result in original French creations.

John Curry, Grant Wood, and I were, in our different ways, trying to Americanize aesthetic attitudes. We felt, as I have said, that we could not get at America with a borrowed point of view. We felt that Parisian aesthetics which denied the value of the subject for painting was denying the only thing which could generate an American form. We were aware of the fact that the great arts of the European motherland itself were arts which were based on subjects carrying public significance. Seeing this, we were not willing to follow the Parisians and equate an apple with a Madonna or with a Midwestern farmer either. We didn't really object to the apple, only to the idea that it could enclose all with which the aesthetic spirit should concern itself. In all of this we were, in one of the characteristic contradictions of our age, on the side of those very Marxist idealists who most criticized us. With the aesthetic tenets of "social realism," we had some pronounced agreements. These tenets were also grounded in public meaning, were opposed to the "decadent formalisms" of Parisian art, and advocated a return to the "significant" subject.

Our Americanist realism was "democratic" rather than "socialist" in the Russian Communist sense, but it aimed to set up a people's art or, more specifically, one which reflected the reality of the American people's life and history in a way which the people could comprehend. We were unwilling to follow the propagandist directions of "socialist realism" because we saw that the actual social conditions which were developing in Russia were not in real accord with its tenets. Realism was realism, we felt, and as such it did not go along with Russian "make-believes" any more than it did with the make-believes of our own plutocracy. However, with the original manifestoes of "socialist realism," in the form outlined by Radek in 1934, we agreed in more ways than we disagreed. Again, if we were not willing to follow the Mexicans Orozco, Rivera, and Siqueiros either ideologically or in terms of form, we were in profound sympathy with their efforts. The vitality of the Mexican art relied, as we wanted ours to, on a return to meaning and the environmental subject. It was, like ours, a repudiation of the Parisian "little emotion." The Mexican art left the privatisms of the modernist movement to take up where Cézanne had left off. It extended the techniques which he developed in reference to nature to an even profounder reference, to that of the human spirit in society. To my mind, it was the only great art of our time. Much of this Mexican art was inspired by the "socialist realism" of the Marxists, but it had the great good fortune to be free of any Russian Marxist dictator.

The Mexican movement and our Americanist one were the only two in this century which made a genuine effort to wrest art from its privatism and return it to a meaningful place in Western society. Both failed to maintain influence. In Mexico today, as in the United States, Parisian modernism rules the minds of the young. This is hard to understand in the case of Mexico with its basic Hispano-Indian folk arts, its general cultural self-sufficiency, and its widespread indigenous creativeness. But it is so. Diego Rivera himself has recorded and protested the fact.

In the United States the reasons for the failure of Regionalism with its Americanist realism are plainer. Unlike that of Mexico, our society provided no popular base for art. Our original Anglo-Protestant civilization was in its nature inimical to art as a theoretic good. Although this spiritual opposition was early contradicted even in Puritan New England—the human soul will not cease to be itself—the grounds for art rested on private luxury rather than public necessity. A luxury of time, time left over from practical efficiencies, was the only thing which excused the creative act; a luxury of surplus wealth was the only thing which could accord it any kind of social position. This hard practicalism was never wholly lived up to. As in the case of New England, that artistic spirit to which Wood, Curry, and I referred for native precedents kept springing up all over the pre-Civil War America. But by and large, and in spite of its many popular supports, it was never able to root itself deeply in our culture.

In the heyday of the new American millionaires of the latter part of the nineteenth century, Art did become, however, a prestige badge of some importance. Fine art was put on a par with golden dishes and floors paved with silver dollars. Nearly always, however, as I have repeatedly emphasized, it was introduced as an import. Any native art was, *ipso facto*, not art. But around the beginning of the century, when new population influences, new wealth, easily won, and newly instituted production relations along with newly urbanized politics began destroying the old moralities of our fathers' Protestantism, art, in a native form, did come to be regarded as a practical good. Not for itself, however. It became good for the rising trade of advertising and an instrument of its hoopla salesmanship which, as business spokesmen said, was in line with the new Protestant image of Christ. Here art found its first real and recognized public function in America. Here also it was degraded as no art has ever been in the history of the world. Along with a fraudulent verbiage, a fraudulent, retouched photograph type of realism was erected which gave to all realism a suggestion of sham. The popular appeals of this stuff also gave to any serious attempts at popularism, such as those inherent in regionalism, a suspicion of venality.

One of the best reasons for the persistence of Parisian modernism in artistic and intellectualist circles in the United States today lies, I believe, in the retreat it provides from the picture horrors of the advertising trade. For the young artist, it provides an especially easy retreat, one which can be made without troublesome discipline and without the need of knowing anything. With such a curse as the advertising game set at the very center of our distributive techniques, in our very life lines, escapist psychologies would be a natural growth in the minds of even the most moderately sensitive men and women. How much more in the case of artists. The reality of advertising's success impels them to a retreat from all reality.

It is perhaps questionable whether any serious publicly directed art of a realistic nature can permanently sustain itself in America as long as the advertising trade in its present form exists. I don't know. A people who is faced with frauds or near frauds, with exaggerated and patently unsustainable claims every time they listen to the radio, watch television, or open a magazine are likely to have their faith in things pretty much undermined. When frauds are presented as realities by all agencies of communication, what is real? Without faith of some kind there can be no background for art; without a belief in the reality of things there can certainly be no background for a realistic art.

It was not, however, the unhappy cultural situations created by the advertising trade alone which broke up the Wood, Curry, and Benton Regionalism. This trade was a contributing cause—it succeeded in corrupting some Regionalist artists, myself at one time, as I have related—but there were other more immediately acute causes operating toward our downfall. In addition to the already listed factors inimical to an indigenous art—colonialism, highbrowism, the make-believes and snobberies of the wealthy circles, on which art was dependent for support, and the general flight from reality which was characteristic of these circles almost from the very end of World War One—some much greater factors arose to assault us. Regionalism was—as I have shown—very largely affirmative of the social explorations of American society and resultant democratic impulses on which President Roosevelt's New Deal was based. The artistic projects of the New Deal were largely sparked by attitudes already affirmed by Wood, Curry, and myself. Roosevelt's early social moves were, as I have said, overwhelmingly Americanist and were concentrated on the solution of specifically American problems. This Americanism found its aesthetic expression in Regionalism. When the world situation began in 1938 and 1939 to inject itself into American politics, and Americans of all classes and of all factions began to realize that our very survival as a nation was being menaced by what was occurring in Europe, American particularisms were pushed into the background and subordinated to the international problem. In this reorientation of our national life and thought, Regionalism was as much out of place as New Dealism itself. It declined in popular interest and lost its grip on the minds of young artists. Shortly after our entrance into the War, what was left of it was turned to a swift and superficial representation of combat and production scenes, to a business of sensational reporting for the popular magazines. There it had its grass-roots substance knocked out.

INDEX

Brown, John, 6
Burchfield, Charles Ephraim, 68, 147
"Business First," 158-60, 168

Cambiaso, Luca, 47
Carles, Arthur, 54
Carlock, John, 16, 18, 19, 21, 24
Carrière, Eugène, 17
Cellini, Benvenuto, 1
Cennini, Cennino, 57
Cézanne, Paul, 16, 21, 22, 23, 30, 33, 35, 37, 43, 51, 76, 181, 182, 183, 184, 185, 186, 189
Chartres, 17, 73
Chase, William Merritt, 12
Chavannes, Puvis de, 56
Chelsea Neighborhood Association, 42, 51
chiaroscuro, 21, 46
Chicago Art Institute, 11
china decorating, 29, 32
Chirico, Giorgio de, 78
Classical art, 16, 39, 76
Clemenceau, Georges, 157
Collarossi, Académie, 16, 19
Communism, 35, 52, 164-72 passim
Constructivism, 43, 148
Copley, John Singleton, 3
Corcoran Gallery, 10
Coughlin, Father Charles Edward, 162
Courbet, Gustave, 17, 154, 180, 183
Craven, Thomas, 29, 54-55, 57
Cubism, 21, 23, 47, 148
Currier and Ives prints, 156
Curry, John Steuart, 1, 6, 70; "Line Storm," 78; and American Regionalism, 147-92 passim; "Kansas Baptism," 155

Dadaism, 40
Daguerre, Louis Jacques Mandé, 180
Daniel, Charles, 39-40; D. Galleries, 39-40, 44, 45, 58

Daughters of the American Revolution, Grant Wood's depiction of, 6
Daumier, Honoré, 180
Davidson, Jo, 18
Davies, Arthur B., 40-41
Debs, Eugene, 52
Delacroix, Ferdinand Victor Eugène, 51, 180
Delaunay, Robert, 34
Delphic Gallery, 61
Derain, André, 35
Dewey, John, 168, 170
Dickinson, Preston, 53
Dodge City, 6
Dôme, Café, 18, 24
Dreiser, Theodore, 160
Duchamps, Marcel, "Nude Descending the Staircase," 78

Eakins, Thomas, 3, 147, 154
Eastman, Max, 169
El Greco (Kyriakos Theotokopoulos), 5, 17, 73; "Nativity," 78
Ernst, Morris, 52
Everett, Dr. John, 65
Expressionism, 40

Fabians, 165
Faulkner, William, 4
Fauves, 21, 148
Feragil Galleries, 173
Force, Mrs. Juliana, 67-68
Fort Lee, New Jersey, 40, 41, 46
Forum Exhibition, the, 37-41 passim, 54
Frank, Jerome, 52; Save America First, 162
Frankfurter, Felix, 52
Frankie and Johnny, 5, 6, 71, 72
Freer, Frederick, W., 12
Friesz, Othon, 35
Frost, Robert, 2

Gauguin, Paul, 23, 183
Ghiberti, Lorenzo, 47
Giotto di Bondone, 56
Gothic art, 153, 176, 180
Goya, Francisco José de, 17

Hart Benton, 58; for the Missouri Capitol, 6, 70, 71, 72, 74; for New York Public Library, 58; for New School of Social Research, 62-67, 70; for the Whitney Museum— "The Arts of Life in America," 67-69, 70, 172; for the Indiana exhibition at the Chicago World's Fair, 69, 70, 71, 152; for the U.S. Treasury Department, 71; for the Truman Library, 74-75
Museum of Modern Art, 78

Nation, Carrie, 6
National Academy, 32
National Gallery, 65
Neo-Fascism, 162
Neo-Impressionism, 19-23 passim, 27, 28, 33, 43, 148
New School for Social Research, 61-67; Benton mural for, 62-67, 70
New York Public Library, 58
Nigger Jim, in Missouri Capitol mural, 6

O'Hara, Mrs., 29, 32
O'Keeffe, Georgia, 45
Orozco, Clemente, 61-63, 68, 171, 189
Orphism, 34
Oswald, Fredrick, 11-13

Pendergast, Boss, in Missouri Capitol mural, 6
Pennsylvania Academy of Art exhibition, 54, 55
People's Art Guild, 35, 36, 42, 44-45, 52, 55
Persephone, 5
Piacenza, Rita, see Benton, Rita Piacenza
Picasso, Pablo, 35; "Lady at Her Toilet," 78
Pierson, Ralph, 62
Pissarro, Camille, 15, 180
Pointillism, 19, 24
Post-Impressionism, 51, 54

Poussin, Nicolas, 22, 37, 181
Prado, 78
Price, Fred, 173

Raabe, Dr. Alfred, 55, 56
Radek, Karl, 52, 189
Raphael, 50
Ray, Man, 40
Reed, Alma, 61-63
Reed, John, 52; Club, 168, 171
Renaissance art, 16, 39, 41, 46, 57, 73, 76, 153, 154, 176, 180, 183, 188
Renoir, Pierre Auguste, 15, 180, 183; "Moulin de la Galette," 15
Rivera, Diego, 68, 170-72, 189
Robinson, Boardman, 51-52, 53, 57, 59
Roman sculpture, 11
Roosevelt, Franklin Delano, 69; at World Economic Conference in London, 1933, 162; and the New Deal, 163, 192
Rubens, Peter Paul, 154, 180
Ruggles, Carl, 54
Ruskin, John, 14, 25
Russell, Morgan, 33

St. Cloud, 20
Salon, Paris, of 1911, 25; spring, 1912, 27
Sandburg, Carl, 2, 5, 163
Sargent, John Singer, 12
Schön, Erhard, 47
Sculpture: Greek, 11; Roman, 11; of Michelangelo, 37, 39; Benton's interest in, 42
Sculptured models: used by Tintoretto, 46-48, 73; used by El Greco, 73; used by Benton, 47-49, 72-74
Seeger, Charles, 54
Siegfried, André, *America Comes of Age*, 159
Signac, Paul, 19
Simonson, Lee, 18
Siqueiros, David Alfaro, 68, 171, 189
Sisley, Alfred, 180